Unshakable

How to Rise, Reset, and Reclaim Your Strength

Even storms bow to steady steps.

By

Dr. Ali Chalhoub

Copyright © 2025 **Dr. Ali Chalhoub**

All rights reserved. No part of this publication may be reproduced, distributed, or transmitted in any form or by any means without the prior written permission of the author.

Dedication

This book is dedicated to every individual who has ever felt lost, overwhelmed, or discouraged. To those who have stumbled and fallen yet found the strength to rise again. To those who have faced seemingly insurmountable obstacles and persevered with unwavering determination. This is a testament to the indomitable human spirit, a celebration of resilience, and a guide for navigating the unpredictable currents of life. It is dedicated to those who dare to keep moving forward, even when the path ahead seems unclear, and to those who are brave enough to embrace the journey, challenges, and all. This book is dedicated to you: a beacon of hope in the face of adversity, a testament to the power within each of us to overcome any obstacle. May it serve as a source of strength, inspiration, and guidance on your unique path to personal growth and fulfillment. It is to you, the reader, who seeks a deeper understanding of self and a stronger connection to your inner resilience, that I offer this book. May it be a catalyst to propel you towards a future brimming with purpose and positivity.

Preface

Life's journey is rarely a smooth, predictable path. Instead, it is often characterized by unexpected twists and turns, moments of triumph and setback, and periods of intense joy and profound sorrow. This book, *Keep Moving Forward*, is born from a deep understanding of this inherent unpredictability and from witnessing the remarkable resilience of the human spirit. As a psychologist and life coach, I've spent years working with individuals navigating a broad spectrum of life challenges. Through these experiences, I've seen firsthand the transformative power of consistent effort, the importance of self-compassion, and the extraordinary capacity we all possess to overcome adversity. This book isn't about avoiding life's inevitable difficulties; it's about learning to navigate them with grace, strength, and unwavering determination. It's a guide to understanding the relentless march of life, building resilience, cultivating self-efficacy, and maintaining momentum, even when the path ahead feels arduous. Inside, you will discover practical strategies, relatable anecdotes, and empowering insights that will help you unlock your inner strength and embrace the journey of personal growth. This is an invitation to embark on a transformative exploration of your capacity for resilience – a journey toward a future filled with purpose, fulfillment, and unwavering hope. I hope the principles and strategies outlined within these pages will provide you with the tools and inspiration not just to survive but to thrive in the face of life's challenges. This is your guide to keep moving forward.

Introduction

Life doesn't wait for us to be ready. It continues its relentless march, presenting us with a constant stream of challenges, opportunities, and unexpected turns. Feeling overwhelmed, discouraged, or lost is a common human experience, yet it doesn't have to define our journey. This book, *UNSHAKABLE*, is your companion on a path toward greater resilience, self-compassion, and personal growth. It's a practical guide that emphasizes the importance of small, consistent steps, reminding you that progress—however incremental—is still progress. We often fall into the trap of waiting for ideal conditions before taking action. However, perfect timing rarely exists. This book encourages you to embrace the journey, acknowledging that life is a process of constant learning, adapting, and growing. Within these pages, you'll discover practical strategies and inspiring stories that demonstrate the power of perseverance.

You'll learn how to identify and overcome limiting beliefs, build resilience, cultivate self-care, and maintain momentum. We'll explore the science behind resilience, the importance of self-compassion, and the transformative power of positive thinking. We will delve into goal-setting, habit formation, and the art of maintaining motivation. The journey of self-discovery and personal growth isn't always easy; it requires consistent effort, self-reflection, and a commitment to keep moving forward. This book will provide you with the map and the tools; you'll supply the courage and determination. Prepare to embark on a transformative journey toward a more resilient, purposeful, and fulfilling life. Let's begin.

Table of Contents

Dedication i

Preface ii

Introduction iii

The Illusion of Control 6

Embracing the Unpredictability 10

The Power of Small Steps 15

Reframing Setbacks as Opportunities 20

Cultivating self-compassion 24

Uncovering Self-Sabotaging Thoughts 29

Challenging Negative Self-Talk 34

Redefining Success on Your Terms 38

Building Self-Efficacy 42

Cultivating a Growth Mindset 46

The Science of Resilience 50

Developing Coping Mechanisms 55

The Importance of Self-Care 59

Seeking Support and Connection 63

Adapting to Change 67

SMART Goal Setting 71

Breaking Down Large Goals 76

Overcoming Procrastination 81

Building Habits for Success 85

Maintaining Motivation 90

Identifying and Challenging Negative Thoughts	94
Cultivating Gratitude	98
Practicing Optimism	102
Visualizing Success	106
Affirmations and Positive Self-Talk	110
The Importance of Self Forgiveness	115
Forgiving Others	120
Letting Go of the Past	124
Breaking Free from Toxic Relationships	129
Embracing Acceptance	133
Identifying Your Values	138
Exploring Your Interests and Talents	142
Setting Meaningful Goals	146
Overcoming Fear and Self-Doubt	151
Creating a Life of Purpose	155
Building Self-Discipline	159
Celebrating Achievements	163
Learning from Setbacks	167
Staying Committed to Your Journey	171
Living a Life of Purpose and Fulfillment	175
Keep Rising	179
Acknowledgments	180
Author Biography	181
Back Cover Blurb for *Unshakable*	182

The Illusion of Control

"You must learn to let go. Release the stress. You were never in control anyway"

Steve Maraboli

We humans are inherently driven by a desire for control. We crave predictability—the comfort of knowing what lies ahead. We meticulously plan our schedules and organize our lives, attempting to orchestrate every detail to minimize uncertainty and maximize our sense of security. We build our lives around the illusion that we are the masters of our destinies, capable of steering clear of every potential obstacle. Yet life, in its magnificent and unpredictable nature, often has other plans.

Imagine a bustling city street, a chaotic symphony of honking horns, screeching tires, and a relentless tide of humanity rushing past. This is a potent metaphor for the relentless march of life itself: a constant flow of events, both expected and unexpected, that sweeps us along, often beyond our conscious control. The unpredictable nature of this "river of life" can be overwhelming, leading to frustration, anxiety, and a sense of powerlessness. We become fixated on trying to control the uncontrollable, struggling against the current rather than learning to navigate it. This relentless pursuit of control, this illusion of mastery, is a primary source of suffering.

The truth is, life is not a perfectly curated garden, meticulously manicured and devoid of weeds or unexpected storms. It is a more rugged landscape, a dynamic interplay of planned actions and unforeseen circumstances. We might carefully lay the groundwork for our dreams, only to find that unanticipated challenges arise: job losses, illnesses, or relationship breakdowns. These elements of unpredictability chip away at our carefully constructed sense of control. It is in these moments of disruption that our resilience is truly tested.

This tendency to seek control isn't inherently harmful; it's a fundamental human need. Our brains are wired to seek patterns, predict outcomes, and create a sense of order in the face of chaos. This striving for control offers a sense of security and the feeling of being in the driver's seat. However, clinging too tightly to this illusion, resisting the inevitable ebb and flow of life, can be profoundly detrimental to our mental and emotional well-being. It leads to increased stress, anxiety, and a heightened sense of frustration when events inevitably deviate from our carefully crafted plans.

The challenge lies not in eliminating the desire for control, but in shifting our perspective. It's about acknowledging the inherent unpredictability of life while simultaneously cultivating an inner resilience that allows us to adapt and thrive despite unforeseen circumstances. It's a matter of learning to dance with life's currents rather than stubbornly fighting against them.

Consider the contrast between the busy city street and a tranquil garden. The street represents chaos and unpredictability, while the garden is a sanctuary of peace, a space where we can cultivate inner calm. The key lies in nurturing that inner peace amidst the external chaos, in finding a sense of equilibrium even when life throws curveballs.

This requires a fundamental shift in perspective, a move away from resisting the unpredictable, and a move toward embracing it. It means acknowledging that while we can influence outcomes through our actions, we cannot entirely control them. Accepting this reality is not about surrendering to fate, but about cultivating a different kind of power, the power of adaptability, the power of resilience, and the power to navigate life's twists and turns with grace and determination.

This journey of relinquishing the illusion of control is not a passive process. It requires active engagement, self-awareness, and a willingness to step outside our comfort zones. It necessitates developing strategies for coping with the unexpected, finding peace amidst the storm, and maintaining our inner equilibrium even when things don't go as planned.

Think about your own life. How often do you find yourself struggling against the inevitable flow of events? How often do you become frustrated when things don't unfold precisely as you envisioned? These are critical self-reflective questions to consider. Identify the areas of your life where you are clinging most tightly to the illusion of control. Are you micromanaging every aspect of your work and becoming anxious over minor details? Are you obsessively controlling your relationships, attempting to dictate the actions and emotions of others? Are you rigidly adhering to a strict schedule and unable to adapt when unforeseen events disrupt your plans?

Understanding the source of this need for control is a significant step toward cultivating greater resilience and adaptability. It's crucial to acknowledge that this need stems from a deep-seated desire for security and predictability, a natural human instinct designed to protect us from perceived threats. However, when this need becomes excessive, it can transform from a source of protection into a source of suffering.

The shift toward embracing the unpredictable isn't about abandoning planning or ceasing to strive for goals. Quite the contrary, it's about creating space for flexibility and adaptation, for responding to unforeseen circumstances with resourcefulness and equanimity, rather than panic and resistance. It means developing a mindset that is both proactive and adaptable, one that understands the limits of our control, while simultaneously celebrating the power of our response.

Consider the metaphor of a river. Fighting against the current, attempting to swim upstream against its relentless force, is exhausting and ultimately futile. The more we struggle, the more energy we expend, and the more exhausted we become. Instead, a more effective approach is to learn to navigate the river, to ride its currents, to understand its rhythms, and to use its flow to your advantage. This is analogous to embracing life's unpredictability and understanding that while we cannot always control the direction of the river, we can learn to navigate its currents with skill and grace.

The journey toward letting go of the illusion of control is not a linear path, it is a process of ongoing learning and adaptation. There will be setbacks, moments when we revert to old habits of control, and moments when we feel overwhelmed by the unpredictable. This is perfectly normal and should not be seen as a sign of failure. The essence lies in our ability to recognize these moments, to reflect on our responses, and to make conscious adjustments along the way. This is the essence of personal growth, the continuous refinement of our ability to navigate the relentless march of life. The ability to both plan and adapt will be critical for our long-term well-being and success. The following section will delve into the power of embracing the unpredictable, highlighting practical strategies to cultivate adaptability, flexibility, and resilience in the face of life's uncertainties.

Embracing the Unpredictability

"Life is what happens to us while we making other plans."

Allen Saunder

We've established the inherent human desire for control, the comfort we find in predictability, and the inevitable frustration that arises when life deviates from our meticulously crafted plans. This yearning for control, while understandable, can become a significant obstacle to our well-being if we allow it to dictate our response to life's unpredictable nature. The question then becomes, how do we reconcile this innate need for security with the reality of life's inherent uncertainty? The answer lies not in suppressing our desire for control, but in shifting our perspective and learning to embrace unpredictability rather than resisting it.

Think of the river again, but this time, imagine yourself not just observing it from the bank, but actively participating in its flow. Picture yourself in a kayak, skillfully navigating its currents, expertly maneuvering around obstacles, and even utilizing the river's energy to propel you forward. Fighting the current would be exhausting, ultimately leading to defeat. Instead, by understanding the river's rhythm, anticipating its changes, and learning to adapt to its unpredictable nature, you can harness its power, making the journey not just survivable, but even exhilarating.

This is the essence of embracing life's unpredictability. It's about recognizing that while we can set our course, we can't completely control the waters we sail upon. Storms will come, unexpected rapids will appear, and the course might shift in ways we didn't anticipate. But instead of succumbing to fear and panic, we learn to navigate these challenges, utilizing our skills, our resilience, and our adaptability to reach our destination.

This doesn't mean abandoning planning altogether. Setting goals, establishing a roadmap, and working towards our aspirations are essential components of a fulfilling life. However, rigid adherence to a predetermined plan, and an inability to adapt when circumstances change, can lead to significant stress and disappointment. The key is to maintain a flexible approach and a willingness to adjust our course as needed, without losing sight of our ultimate destination.

Consider the entrepreneur launching a new business. A detailed business plan is crucial, outlining the steps necessary for success. However, the market might shift unexpectedly, competition might be fiercer than anticipated, or unforeseen circumstances might arise that disrupt the initial plan. The entrepreneur who clings rigidly to the original plan, refusing to adapt to changing conditions, is far less likely to succeed than one who remains flexible, capable of pivoting when necessary, and who views unforeseen challenges not as obstacles, but as opportunities for innovation and growth.

In the same way, think about relationships. We may have expectations and hopes for how a relationship will unfold, but rigid adherence to these expectations can stifle spontaneity and adaptability, leading to conflict and disappointment. Embracing the unpredictability in relationships requires a willingness to accept that our partners may change, that challenges will arise, and that the journey will not always be smooth. The ability to navigate these challenges together, and to adapt to changing circumstances, is key to building strong, resilient relationships.

This concept extends to virtually every aspect of life. From career trajectories to personal growth, from financial stability to physical health, the unexpected is inevitable. The key to navigating these complexities lies not in resisting the unpredictable, but in cultivating the skills necessary to embrace adaptability, flexibility, and resilience.

Adaptability is the ability to adjust to changing circumstances. It's about possessing a mindset that is not resistant to change, but embraces it as an opportunity for learning and growth. It involves developing a range of coping mechanisms, strategies for problem-solving, and the ability to see challenges as opportunities for creative solutions.

Flexibility is the capacity to alter our plans and expectations when necessary. It's about letting go of rigid adherence to predetermined outcomes, and instead maintaining a sense of openness to possibilities. It's about recognizing that our initial plans might need revision, and being willing to embrace new directions.

Resilience, the ability to bounce back from setbacks, is the most critical element of embracing unpredictability. It's about cultivating a mindset of perseverance, a belief in our ability to overcome challenges, and a capacity to learn from our mistakes. It involves developing a support system of friends, family, and mentors who can offer encouragement and guidance during difficult times.

Cultivating these qualities of adaptability, flexibility, and resilience isn't a passive process. It requires conscious effort, self-reflection, and a commitment to personal growth. It involves actively seeking opportunities to step outside our comfort zones, to challenge our assumptions, and to embrace new experiences. This might involve taking risks, learning new skills, seeking out new perspectives, and actively cultivating self-compassion.

Self-compassion is crucial. When faced with unexpected challenges, it's easy to fall into self-criticism and self-doubt. However, practicing self-compassion and treating ourselves with the same kindness and understanding we would offer a friend in a similar situation is essential for building resilience and navigating the unpredictable nature of life.

Think about incorporating mindfulness practices into your daily routine. Mindfulness encourages a present-moment awareness, helping us to remain grounded and centered amidst the chaos of life. It helps us to observe our thoughts and emotions without judgment, allowing us to respond to challenges with greater clarity and equanimity.

Regular exercise, healthy eating habits, and sufficient sleep are also vital for building resilience. These practices nourish our physical and mental well-being, providing us with the energy and strength we need to cope with life's inevitable challenges. Building a strong support system and fostering meaningful connections with family and friends can provide a buffer against stress and adversity, offering a sense of belonging and shared experience.

Ultimately, embracing the unpredictability of life is not about abandoning our goals or ceasing to strive for our aspirations. Instead, it's about developing the skills and mindset needed to navigate the journey, to adapt to changing circumstances, and to emerge stronger and wiser from every challenge we encounter. It's about recognizing that life's relentless march is not something to be feared, but a journey to be embraced, with all its twists, turns, and unexpected detours. It's about learning to dance with the current, finding grace and strength in the flow of life itself. This is the path to a more resilient, more fulfilling, and ultimately more meaningful life. The journey toward this acceptance is a continuous process, requiring ongoing self-reflection, adaptation, and an unwavering commitment to personal growth. It is a lifelong journey, not a destination, and the rewards are immeasurable.

Now that we've learned to ride the unpredictable currents of life, the next question is, how do we move forward, one step at a time?

The Power of Small Steps

> *"The journey of a thousand miles begins with a single step"*
>
> Lao Tzu

We've explored the unpredictable nature of life and the importance of adaptability, flexibility, and resilience in navigating its currents. But how do we actually apply these principles in our daily lives, particularly when faced with overwhelming challenges? The answer lies in the power of small steps.

Imagine you're faced with a monumental task, something that seems so immense, so daunting, that it paralyzes you before you even begin. Perhaps it's a significant personal goal, like writing a novel, starting a business, or overcoming a deep-seated fear. Or maybe it's a more practical challenge, like paying off debt, improving your health, or repairing a strained relationship. The sheer scale of these objectives can feel overwhelming, leading to inaction and, ultimately, to disappointment.

This is where the power of small steps comes into play. Forget the grand gestures and sweeping pronouncements of immediate change. Instead, focus on the tiny, incremental advancements, the seemingly insignificant actions that, when compounded over time, lead to remarkable progress.

Think of climbing a mountain. Reaching the summit isn't achieved with one giant leap. Instead, it's a series of small, consistent steps, each one bringing you closer to your goal. There will be steep inclines, rocky paths, and moments of exhaustion and doubt. But with each step, however small, you are undeniably moving forward. You are gaining altitude, inching closer to your destination. The view from the summit is breathtaking, but it's the accumulation of countless small steps that gets you there.

Similarly, significant personal growth and achievement are rarely the result of sudden breakthroughs or overnight transformations. They are the product of consistent, persistent effort, a series of small, deliberate actions taken day after day, week after week, month after month. These small steps might seem insignificant in isolation, but their cumulative effect is transformative.

Consider the writer struggling to complete a novel. The task of writing an entire book can seem utterly overwhelming. But what if, instead of focusing on the daunting prospect of finishing the entire manuscript, the writer focuses on a smaller, more manageable goal, like writing just one page a day? This seemingly insignificant task is easily achievable, even on days when motivation is low. Yet, over time, these small daily contributions accumulate, eventually leading to the completion of the novel.

Or consider the individual striving to improve their physical fitness. The goal of losing weight or building strength can feel daunting. But starting with a 15-minute walk each day, gradually increasing the duration and intensity over time, is a far more achievable and sustainable approach than attempting a grueling workout regimen from the outset. The consistency of the small steps is what creates lasting change.

The power of small steps lies not just in their achievability, but also in their ability to build momentum. Each small victory, each incremental accomplishment, reinforces a sense of progress, fueling motivation and fostering a sense of self-efficacy. This positive feedback loop is crucial for sustaining effort over the long term. The more small steps you take, the stronger your belief in your ability to achieve your goals.

This isn't about setting low standards or accepting mediocrity. It's about employing a strategic approach to achieving significant goals, recognizing that consistent, incremental progress is far more effective than sporadic bursts of intense effort that often burn out quickly.

One of the common pitfalls in pursuing ambitious goals is the tendency to focus solely on the result, losing sight of the process. We become so fixated on the summit that we overlook the importance of each step along the way. This can lead to discouragement and, ultimately, to giving up.

By focusing on the small steps, we shift our attention from the overwhelming magnitude of the overall goal to the manageable task at hand. This helps us to maintain motivation, to celebrate small victories, and to build momentum toward ultimate success.

Think of it like building a house. You wouldn't attempt to build the entire house in a single day. Instead, you would focus on completing smaller, more manageable tasks, such as laying the foundation, framing the walls, and installing the roof. Each step is essential, and each step brings you closer to the completion of the project. The same principle applies to achieving any significant goal.

The beauty of small steps is that they can be tailored to individual circumstances. There's no one-size-fits-all approach. The key is to identify the smallest, most achievable action you can take toward your goal, and then take it. Even if it seems insignificant, it's still progress. And consistent progress, however small, ultimately leads to significant achievement.

Consider the individual struggling with debt. Instead of feeling overwhelmed by the total amount owed, they could focus on a small, manageable goal of paying off a portion of the debt each month. This consistent effort, however small, will eventually lead to debt reduction and, ultimately, financial freedom.

Or consider the individual seeking to improve a strained relationship. Instead of expecting an immediate transformation, they could focus on small acts of kindness and communication, such as sending a text message, making a phone call, or initiating a conversation. These small gestures, repeated consistently, can gradually repair the relationship.

The power of small steps lies in their ability to build momentum, create positive feedback loops, and foster a sense of accomplishment. They help us to break down daunting tasks into manageable chunks, to maintain motivation, and to celebrate small victories along the way. The accumulation of these small steps, over time, leads to remarkable achievements.

This approach is not about minimizing our ambitions or settling for less. It is about acknowledging the reality of the process, recognizing that significant progress is often the product of countless small actions taken consistently over time. It is about cultivating patience, perseverance, and a belief in the power of small, consistent effort.

Remember, every journey, no matter how long or challenging, begins with a single step. And it is the consistent repetition of these steps, the accumulation of these small victories, that ultimately leads to the destination. Embrace the power of small steps, and you will unlock the potential for extraordinary achievements in every aspect of your life. The journey might be extended, the path might be winding, but with consistent, small steps, you will inevitably reach your destination. The key is not to focus on the immensity of the goal, but on the small, manageable steps required to reach it. And remember, even the most minor step forward is still progress. Keep moving forward, one step at a time. The path to success is paved with these seemingly insignificant steps, each one a testament to your dedication and commitment.

Reframing Setbacks as Opportunities

We've established the importance of consistent, incremental progress, of taking those seemingly insignificant steps that, when accumulated, lead to remarkable achievements. But what happens when the relentless march of life throws a curveball? What happens when we stumble and face setbacks that threaten to derail our progress entirely? This is where the crucial skill of reframing setbacks as opportunities comes into play.

Setbacks are inevitable. They are a fundamental part of the human experience. No journey, no matter how well planned, is devoid of obstacles. Whether it's a missed deadline at work, a relationship falling apart, a health challenge, or a financial setback, these experiences can feel devastating, leaving us questioning our abilities and our future. The natural human response is often to retreat, to withdraw, to allow the disappointment to consume us. But this is precisely where the opportunity for growth lies.

The key to navigating setbacks lies in our perspective. Instead of viewing them as failures, as evidence of our shortcomings, we must learn to see them as valuable learning experiences, as opportunities for personal development and transformation. This shift in perspective is crucial for maintaining momentum and continuing the relentless march forward.

Consider the athlete who suffers a serious injury. This is undoubtedly a setback, a significant disruption to their training regimen, their competition schedule, and their aspirations. The initial response is likely to be one of despair, of questioning whether their career is over. But for those who persevere, the injury becomes an opportunity for growth. It forces them to re-evaluate their training methods, address underlying weaknesses, and develop a deeper understanding of their body and its limits. The recovery process becomes a journey of self-discovery, leading to a stronger, more resilient athlete, often returning to competition even more determined and focused.

Think of the artist struggling with creative block. The inability to produce new work and the frustration of staring at a blank canvas or screen can be incredibly disheartening. The impulse is to give up, to believe that their creative well has run dry. However, this perceived failure can be the catalyst for innovation. It can force the artist to explore new techniques, experiment with different styles, and find inspiration in unexpected places. The struggle becomes a source of creativity, eventually leading to a breakthrough and a richer, more nuanced artistic expression.

These examples demonstrate the power of reframing setbacks. They illustrate how challenges, while painful, can be transformed into opportunities for personal and professional growth. This isn't about denying the difficulty or minimizing the pain. It's about recognizing the potential for learning and development within those experiences.

One of the most effective strategies for reframing setbacks is to analyze them objectively. Instead of dwelling on the negative emotions associated with the setback, take some time to reflect on what happened, what went wrong, and what lessons can be learned. What were the contributing factors? What could you have done differently? This analytical approach helps to distance yourself from the emotional turmoil, allowing you to see the situation with greater clarity and objectivity.

Another helpful strategy is to focus on what you can control. Setbacks often involve elements beyond our control, such as unforeseen circumstances, the actions of others, and unexpected events. While acknowledging these factors is essential, dwelling on them only serves to increase feelings of helplessness and despair. Instead, concentrate on the aspects of the situation that are within your control. What steps can you take to mitigate the damage, to prevent similar setbacks in the future, or to learn from the experience?

Furthermore, it's crucial to develop a growth mindset. This involves viewing challenges as opportunities for learning and development, rather than as evidence of personal failings. Individuals with a growth mindset believe that their abilities and intelligence can be developed through dedication and hard work. They embrace challenges, learn from mistakes, and persist in the face of setbacks. This perspective is crucial for reframing setbacks as opportunities for growth.

It is also important to cultivate self-compassion. Setbacks can be challenging to cope with, and it's natural to experience feelings of disappointment, frustration, or even self-blame. However, self-criticism only compounds the problem, hindering our ability to learn and move forward. Instead, treat yourself with kindness and understanding, acknowledging that everyone faces setbacks and that mistakes are a part of the learning process.

The process of reframing a setback into an opportunity is not always easy. It requires conscious effort, self-reflection, and a willingness to confront uncomfortable emotions. However, by embracing this process, we can transform challenges into catalysts for personal growth, strengthening our resilience and deepening our understanding of ourselves and the world around us.

Consider the entrepreneur who launches a business only to see it fail within the first year. The initial reaction might be devastation and self-doubt. However, a successful entrepreneur will dissect the failure by analyzing the market conditions, their business model, and their performance. They'll identify areas for improvement, learn from their mistakes, and use this experience to inform their next venture. The failed business becomes a valuable learning experience, paving the way for future success. This isn't to say that they won't feel the pain of the failure, but they understand that failure is not the end, but a stepping stone.

The path to achieving our goals is rarely a straight line, it's more like a winding road filled with unexpected twists, turns, and obstacles. Setbacks are inevitable, but our response to them defines our character and, ultimately, our success. By choosing to reframe setbacks as opportunities for growth, we transform challenges into stepping stones, turning potential derailments into catalysts for personal and professional development. This is the essence of resilience, the ability to not only withstand adversity but to emerge from it stronger and wiser. This isn't a passive acceptance of hardship; it's an active, conscious choice to learn, adapt, and grow from every experience, no matter how difficult. It's about embracing the relentless march of life, accepting its unpredictable nature, and understanding that even in the midst of adversity, the potential for growth and progress remains. And it's through this consistent progress, this unwavering commitment to moving forward, even after setbacks, that we achieve our full potential. The journey may be challenging, but the rewards of resilience and growth are immeasurable. Keep moving forward. Even setbacks are stepping stones to success.

Pause and Reflect: Setbacks often arrive uninvited, but they carry lessons we wouldn't otherwise learn.

Ask yourself: What recent setback have you experienced, and what lesson might it hold for you? Write it down! Don't rush the answer. Sometimes, clarity comes when we're honest enough to sit with the discomfort.

Cultivating self-compassion

We've explored the power of reframing setbacks as opportunities for growth, acknowledging the inevitable bumps and detours on life's relentless journey. However, even with the most effective reframing strategies, the emotional toll of setbacks can be significant. This is where the crucial role of self-compassion comes into play. Self-compassion isn't about self-indulgence or avoiding responsibility, it's about treating yourself with the same kindness, understanding, and acceptance that you would offer a close friend facing similar challenges.

Imagine a friend confiding in you about a challenging experience, a job loss, a relationship breakdown, or a personal failure. What would your response be? Would you rebuke them, pointing out their flaws and mistakes? Likely not. You would probably offer words of comfort, empathy, and understanding, reminding them of their strengths, their resilience, and their inherent worth. This is the essence of self-compassion, extending that same kindness and understanding to yourself.

Cultivating self-compassion is a vital skill for navigating the relentless march of life. When faced with setbacks, it's natural to experience feelings of self-criticism, self-doubt, and even self-blame. This inner critic, often harsh and unforgiving, can amplify the negative emotions associated with setbacks, hindering our ability to learn, grow, and move forward. Self-compassion offers a powerful antidote to this negative self-talk, providing a buffer against the harshness of self-criticism and fostering a sense of self-acceptance and resilience.

One of the key components of self-compassion is self-kindness. This involves treating yourself with the same empathy and understanding that you would offer a friend in need. Instead of dwelling on your mistakes and shortcomings, acknowledge your struggles with compassion, recognizing that everyone makes mistakes and experiences setbacks. When you stumble, offer yourself the same kindness and support that you would readily give to someone you care about. This doesn't mean ignoring the problem or avoiding responsibility; it means acknowledging your pain and offering yourself comfort rather than judgment.

Another crucial element of self-compassion is recognizing that you are not alone in your suffering. Setbacks, challenges, and imperfections are a universal human experience. Everyone faces difficulties, struggles, and moments of failure. Recognizing this shared humanity helps to alleviate feelings of isolation and shame, reminding you that you are not unique in your experience and that your struggles are valid and understandable. Connecting with others who have faced similar challenges can be immensely helpful in fostering a sense of shared experience and reducing feelings of isolation.

Finally, mindfulness plays a crucial role in cultivating self-compassion. Mindfulness involves paying attention to the present moment without judgment. When you're feeling overwhelmed by negative emotions, take a moment to observe them without getting swept away by them. Acknowledge your feelings without trying to suppress or ignore them. This mindful awareness allows you to approach your struggles with greater clarity and compassion, fostering a sense of self-acceptance and understanding.

Here are some practical exercises to help you cultivate self-compassion:

The Self-Compassion Break: When you are feeling overwhelmed by negative emotions, find a quiet space and gently place a hand over your heart. Silently repeat the following phrases: "This is a moment of suffering," "Suffering is a part of life," and "May I be kind to myself." Allow yourself to feel the warmth of your hand and the comforting words. This simple exercise can help to soothe your emotional pain and cultivate a sense of self-acceptance.

The Compassionate Letter: Write a letter to yourself as if you were a compassionate friend offering support and encouragement.

Acknowledge your struggles, validate your feelings, and offer words of kindness, understanding, and reassurance. This exercise can be beneficial in addressing feelings of self-criticism and self-doubt.

Mindful Self-Reflection: Take some time each day to reflect on your thoughts and feelings without judgment. Notice any patterns of self-criticism or negative self-talk. When you identify these patterns, gently challenge them with compassionate self-statements.

For example, instead of thinking, "I'm such a failure," you might say, "I'm having a difficult time right now, but this doesn't define me. Everyone faces setbacks."

Practice Gratitude: Focusing on what you're grateful for, even in the midst of difficulties, can shift your perspective and cultivate feelings of self-worth and appreciation. Take time each day to reflect on the positive aspects of your life, no matter how small they may seem.

Engage in Self-Care: Self-compassion is not just about emotional support. It also encompasses physical self-care. Ensure you're prioritizing your physical and mental well-being by getting enough sleep, eating nutritious food, exercising regularly, and engaging in activities that bring you joy and relaxation. Neglecting your physical health will only exacerbate emotional difficulties.

Cultivating self-compassion is an ongoing process, not a destination. It requires consistent practice and a willingness to treat yourself with the same kindness and understanding that you would offer a friend. By incorporating these exercises into your daily routine, you'll gradually develop a greater capacity for self-compassion, enabling you to navigate life's challenges with greater resilience, grace, and inner peace. Remember, self-compassion isn't a sign of weakness, it's a sign of strength, a recognition of your inherent worth, and a commitment to your well-being.

It's important to understand that self-compassion isn't about ignoring your mistakes or avoiding responsibility. It's about acknowledging your imperfections and struggles with kindness and understanding, learning from your experiences, and moving forward with greater self-acceptance. It's about recognizing that setbacks are a natural part of life and that they don't diminish your inherent worth.

Think of it this way: would you berate a friend for making a mistake? Probably not. You would offer support, understanding, and encouragement. Self-compassion is about extending that same level of kindness and understanding to yourself. It's about recognizing that everyone makes mistakes and that imperfections are part of the human experience.

Furthermore, self-compassion can significantly impact your ability to cope with stress. When faced with challenging situations, individuals with high levels of self-compassion are better able to manage their emotional responses, reducing feelings of anxiety, depression, and overwhelm. They are also more likely to seek support from others and engage in healthy coping mechanisms.

The benefits of self-compassion extend beyond stress management. Studies have shown a strong correlation between self-compassion and increased self-esteem, improved resilience, and enhanced overall well-being. Individuals who practice self-compassion are more likely to set realistic goals, persevere in the face of setbacks, and maintain a positive outlook on life.

They are also more likely to engage in healthy behaviors that support their physical and mental health.

The relentless march of life often throws unexpected challenges our way. While reframing setbacks is crucial, self-compassion acts as a vital support system, providing emotional resilience and a foundation for navigating adversity. Remember, the journey is not always smooth, and it's okay to stumble. What matters is that you get back up, treat yourself with kindness, and continue moving forward. The consistent practice of self-compassion will equip you with the emotional tools to navigate life's challenges with greater strength, understanding, and unwavering self-belief. Embrace the journey, embrace your imperfections, and embrace the power of self-compassion. It's a journey worth undertaking. It's a journey toward a more fulfilling and compassionate life.

The Pillars of Self-Compassion

1. *Self-kindness: Speak to yourself with the same warmth and understanding you'd offer a friend. Replace harsh self-criticism with patience and care.*
2. *Shared Humanity: Remember that pain, failure, and imperfection are part of the human experience. You are not alone in your struggles.*
3. *Mindfulness: Be present with your thoughts and feelings without judgment. Awareness opens the door to healing.*

Uncovering Self-Sabotaging Thoughts

We've established the vital role of self-compassion in navigating life's inevitable setbacks. However, even with self-compassion as a bedrock, persistent negative thought patterns can significantly impede our progress. These are the limiting beliefs we must confront, the internal saboteurs whispering doubts and hindering our forward momentum. Identifying and challenging these self-sabotaging thoughts is crucial to unlocking our full potential and maintaining our forward progress.

Our minds, while powerful tools, are also prone to cognitive distortions and systematic errors in thinking that can lead to inaccurate interpretations of reality. These distortions often fuel negative emotions and self-defeating behaviors, creating a cycle that reinforces limiting beliefs. Understanding these common cognitive distortions is the first step in breaking free from their grip.

One prevalent cognitive distortion is **catastrophizing**, the tendency to magnify the potential negative consequences of a situation. Instead of realistically assessing the possibilities, we envision the worst-case scenario, often with disproportionate fear and anxiety. For example, imagine missing a deadline at work. A realistic assessment might involve addressing the situation with your supervisor, setting a plan to catch up, and accepting potential consequences. However, catastrophizing might lead to thoughts like, "I'm going to lose my job. My career is ruined. I'll never find another position." This exaggerated and unrealistic fear paralyzes us, hindering our ability to take constructive action.

Another common distortion is **all-or-nothing thinking**, also known as black-and-white thinking. This involves seeing situations in extreme terms, with no middle ground. Success is viewed as absolute perfection, and any imperfection is considered complete failure. For instance, a presentation that receives primarily positive feedback might be dismissed because of one critical comment. The focus shifts entirely to the negative aspect, overlooking the overall success. This can be devastating to self-esteem and can lead to avoidance of future opportunities for fear of failure.

Overgeneralization involves drawing broad, sweeping conclusions based on limited evidence. A single negative experience might be seen as representative of future occurrences. For instance, if a job application is rejected, an overgeneralization might be, "I'm never going to find a job," completely dismissing the possibility of success in future applications. This distortion prevents us from learning from mistakes and fuels feelings of hopelessness and defeat.

Filtering involves selectively focusing on negative aspects while ignoring positive ones. This leads to a skewed perception of reality, magnifying flaws and minimizing strengths. Imagine receiving positive feedback on a project but focusing solely on a tiny criticism. This filtering process prevents you from appreciating the overall success and reinforces negative self-perception.

Personalization involves taking responsibility for events outside your control. It's the tendency to assume that you are the cause of adverse events, even when there's no evidence to support this conclusion. For instance, a friend canceling plans might be interpreted as a personal rejection, completely overlooking other potential reasons for the cancellation. This unnecessary self-blame perpetuates feelings of guilt and inadequacy.

Should **statements** impose rigid expectations on ourselves and others, creating pressure and leading to self-criticism when these expectations aren't met. Statements like "I should be more organized" or "I should have handled that differently" create unnecessary self-judgment. These demands, often unrealistic, breed self-criticism and hinder self-acceptance.

Emotional reasoning involves mistaking feelings for facts. This occurs when we allow our emotions to dictate our perception of reality. For example, feeling anxious about a public speaking engagement might lead to the conclusion of "I'm going to fail," based purely on the feeling of anxiety, irrespective of any evidence. This conflation of feelings and reality obstructs objective self-assessment and action.

Identifying these cognitive distortions is a crucial first step in overcoming them. However, simply recognizing these patterns isn't enough. Instead, we need practical strategies to challenge and reframe these self-sabotaging thoughts.

One effective technique is when you catch yourself catastrophizing, for example, ask yourself: "What is the evidence that this worst-case scenario will actually happen? What are the more likely outcomes? What steps can I take to mitigate the risks?" By challenging the exaggerated nature of the thought, you begin to detach from its emotional grip.

Another helpful strategy is to **reframe negative thoughts into more balanced and realistic perspectives**. Instead of focusing on what went wrong, try to identify what you learned from the experience and how you can improve in the future. This shift in perspective encourages growth and resilience instead of fostering feelings of defeat.

Journaling can be a powerful tool in uncovering and challenging these distorted thoughts. I'd like you to regularly write down your thoughts and feelings, paying attention to the patterns that emerge from them.

Identify the cognitive distortions present and then actively challenge them by writing down more balanced and realistic interpretations.

Cognitive restructuring involves systematically replacing negative thoughts with more positive and realistic ones. This process requires consistent effort and practice, but the rewards are well worth the investment. Regular practice helps to establish new, more constructive thought patterns, gradually reducing the influence of negative self-talk.

Here's a quick reference table summarizing some common thinking distortions and how to reframe them:

Cognitive Distortion	Example Thought	Reframe Strategy
All-or-Nothing	"I failed once, so I'm a failure."	"One setback doesn't define my entire ability."
Overgeneralization	"This always happens to me."	"This happened once. That doesn't mean it always will."
Mental Filtering	"I made one mistake, so everything is ruined."	"Yes, I made a mistake—but I also did a lot right."
Catastrophizing	"If I mess this up, everything is over."	"Mistakes are part of learning. I can handle it."
Personalization	"It's all my fault."	"There were many factors involved—it's not all on me."

It is important to remember that challenging these deeply ingrained thought patterns takes time and persistence. It's not about magically erasing negative thoughts, but about gradually building a more balanced and realistic perspective. Setbacks are inevitable; however, with consistent self-awareness and the willingness to challenge these cognitive distortions, we can significantly reduce their impact on our emotional well-being and enhance our ability to maintain forward momentum. This consistent effort to identify and reframe these negative thoughts is a crucial component in building resilience and ensuring our continued progress on life's journey.

Please feel free to seek professional guidance from a therapist or counselor. They can provide personalized support and techniques to identify and effectively manage these thought patterns. Their expertise can prove invaluable in navigating the intricacies of your thought processes and developing effective coping strategies.

Remember, the path to personal growth is a continuous journey, and setbacks are inevitable. However, by understanding and actively challenging our self-sabotaging thoughts, we equip ourselves with the tools to navigate these challenges with greater resilience and maintain our forward momentum, even amidst adversity. The key lies in consistently cultivating self-awareness, challenging distorted thoughts, and replacing negativity with a more realistic and compassionate self-perception. The relentless march of life continues, and with conscious effort, we can continue to move forward, stronger and more resilient than ever.

Challenging Negative Self-Talk

Building upon our understanding of cognitive distortions and their impact on our progress, let's now delve into the practical application of replacing negative self-talk with positive affirmations and self-encouraging statements. This shift from negativity to positivity is not about ignoring reality or creating a false sense of optimism, instead, it's about consciously cultivating a more balanced and supportive inner dialogue that fuels our resilience and propels us forward.

Negative self-talk, as we've explored, often operates on autopilot, a deeply ingrained habit of mind that requires conscious effort to interrupt and redirect. This involves more than simply replacing a negative thought with a positive one, it requires a deeper understanding of the underlying beliefs fueling that negativity. Let's say, for example, you consistently tell yourself, "I'm not good enough." This isn't just a fleeting thought, it's a deeply held belief that shapes your actions and perceptions. To effectively counter this, we must examine the origins of this belief. What experiences shaped this conviction? Was it a critical parent, a past failure, or a string of perceived rejections? Identifying the roots allows us to approach the belief with empathy and understanding, rather than simply trying to force a positive statement onto it.

Once you've identified the source of the negative belief, you can begin to challenge its validity. Ask yourself: Is this belief genuinely accurate? Is there evidence to support it? Or is it based on limited experiences, skewed perceptions, or outdated interpretations? Often, we cling to negative self-beliefs because they feel familiar, even if they're not serving us. The process of challenging these beliefs is akin to gently but firmly questioning an old friend who consistently provides unhelpful advice. You appreciate their presence, but recognize that their influence is detrimental to your well-being.

Replacing negative self-talk with positive affirmations requires a delicate balance. Avoid generic, overly enthusiastic affirmations that feel inauthentic. Instead, create statements that resonate with your values and aspirations. The goal isn't to deceive yourself, but to gently nurture a more self-compassionate and encouraging inner voice. For example, instead of "I am perfect," which is unrealistic and potentially self-defeating, try "I am worthy of love and respect, and I am continually growing and learning." This statement acknowledges imperfections while fostering a sense of self-acceptance and progress.

The process of cultivating positive self-talk is ongoing, requiring consistent practice and patience. It's not a quick fix, but a gradual shift in mindset. Think of it as training a muscle; the more you exercise it, the stronger it becomes. Start with small, manageable changes. Instead of attempting to transform your inner dialogue overnight, focus on identifying and replacing just one or two negative thoughts each day. Over time, this consistent effort will yield significant results, fostering a more positive and empowering internal landscape.

Techniques like mindful awareness can be incredibly helpful in interrupting negative thought patterns. When you notice a negative thought arising, don't judge yourself for having it; acknowledge its presence without getting carried away by it. Observe the thought as a fleeting cloud in the sky, rather than a storm that defines your entire being. This detached observation allows you to create space between yourself and the thought, reducing its power over you.

Combining mindful awareness with positive affirmations creates a powerful synergy. As you become more aware of your negative thoughts, actively replace them with positive, self-encouraging statements. This isn't about suppressing negative emotions. It's about gently redirecting your focus toward a more constructive and supportive inner narrative. Remember, the goal is not to eliminate all negativity, but to cultivate a more balanced perspective where positive self-talk outweighs negative self-criticism.

To further enhance this practice, let's explore a guided meditation designed to cultivate positive self-talk and reduce the impact of negative thoughts. Find a quiet space where you can sit or lie down comfortably. Close your eyes gently and begin to focus on your breath, noticing the natural rhythm of inhalation and exhalation. As you breathe, allow your body to relax, releasing any tension you may be holding.

Now, bring your attention to your thoughts. Take note of any opposing thoughts or self-criticisms that arise. Don't judge these thoughts, simply observe them without getting carried away. Imagine these thoughts as clouds drifting across the sky. They appear, remain for a while, and then drift away.

Next, begin to repeat a positive affirmation silently to yourself. Choose an affirmation that resonates with you, such as "I am capable," "I am worthy," or "I am strong." Repeat this affirmation with each breath, allowing it to fill your mind and heart. Feel the sense of peace and self-acceptance that this affirmation brings.

Continue this practice for several minutes, allowing the positive affirmation to gently replace the negative thoughts. As you become more familiar with this technique, you can extend the duration of the meditation and incorporate new affirmations.

When you're ready, gently open your eyes and bring your awareness back to your surroundings. Carry a sense of peace and self-acceptance with you throughout the day. Remember, this meditation is a tool to help you cultivate positive self-talk. Practice regularly, and you will gradually notice a positive shift in your inner dialogue.

The power of positive self-talk extends beyond simply feeling better; it has a profound impact on our actions and achievements. When we speak to ourselves with kindness and encouragement, we build confidence, resilience, and motivation. This inner strength fuels our ability to overcome challenges, persist in the face of setbacks, and achieve our goals. It allows us to approach tasks with a sense of possibility rather than fear or self-doubt.

Positive self-talk isn't a magical solution to all our problems, but it is a powerful tool in our arsenal for personal growth and well-being. It's an investment in our emotional health, fostering a supportive inner environment where we can nurture our strengths, learn from our mistakes, and cultivate a more fulfilling life. Remember, the journey toward positive self-talk is a continuous process, a journey of self-discovery and self-acceptance. Be patient with yourself, celebrate your progress, and continue to nurture that positive inner voice that whispers of your strength, resilience, and potential.

In conclusion, consistently challenging negative self-talk and replacing it with positive affirmations is a journey, not a destination. It's about building a healthier, more supportive internal dialogue that empowers you to navigate life's challenges with greater resilience and maintain the momentum necessary to keep moving forward. This conscious effort to cultivate self-compassion and positive self-perception is a critical step in unlocking your full potential and living a life aligned with your values and aspirations. The relentless march of life continues; let your positive self-talk be the steady drumbeat guiding your progress forward.

Redefining Success on Your Terms

We've spent considerable time examining the insidious nature of limiting beliefs and the detrimental effect of negative self-talk. We've learned how to identify these internal saboteurs, challenge their validity, and begin replacing them with more constructive, self-affirming statements. This process, while challenging, is foundational to unlocking your true potential and maintaining the momentum to keep moving forward. But the journey toward a fulfilling life extends beyond simply silencing the inner critic. It requires a fundamental shift in how we perceive and define success itself.

Society bombards us with images and narratives of "success," often portraying it as a singular, unattainable ideal: a luxurious lifestyle, a high-powered career, a picture-perfect family. This narrow definition of success, perpetuated by media and cultural norms, sets an unrealistic standard, leading many to feel inadequate and perpetually falling short. This feeling of inadequacy isn't a reflection of personal failings, but a consequence of comparing ourselves to an artificially constructed ideal, often divorced from our unique values and aspirations.

The pressure to conform to externally imposed definitions of success can be overwhelming, fostering a sense of dissatisfaction and anxiety, even when objectively, we've achieved significant milestones. We might feel successful by societal standards with a prestigious job, a large house, and material wealth, yet remain deeply unfulfilled. This disconnect arises from the fundamental mismatch between externally imposed expectations and our internal sense of purpose and fulfillment.

Redefining success on your terms is not about rejecting achievement or minimizing ambition, instead, it's about aligning your pursuits with your authentic self. It's about recognizing that success is a deeply personal and multifaceted concept, not a monolithic entity to be chased and captured. What constitutes success for one individual might be entirely irrelevant to another.

Consider, for example, the individual who prioritizes family and community above material possessions. Their definition of success might involve raising a loving family, contributing to their community through volunteer work, and fostering meaningful relationships. For them, the measure of success isn't a hefty bank account, but the richness of their connections and the positive impact they have on the lives of others. This isn't a lesser form of success. It's a different, equally valid path.

Then there's the artist who sacrifices financial stability to pursue their creative passions. Their definition of success isn't measured by financial wealth, but by the fulfillment derived from expressing their creativity, connecting with their audience, and leaving a lasting artistic legacy. The pursuit of art might not align with conventional definitions of success, but it represents a genuine expression of their values and a unique path toward fulfillment.

Similarly, an entrepreneur who dedicates their life to building a sustainable and socially responsible business might measure success not solely by profit margins, but by the positive impact their business has on the environment and the community. This type of success is often more meaningful and lasting, even if it deviates from the traditional measures of wealth accumulation.

These examples highlight the crucial role of individual values in shaping our understanding of success. It's not about abandoning ambition or setting low expectations. Instead, it's about aligning our ambitions with what truly matters to us. Ask yourself, what are your core values? What brings you genuine joy and fulfillment? What legacy do you wish to leave behind?

Understanding and prioritizing your values is the foundation of redefining success on your terms. Once you have a clear understanding of your values, you can begin to align your goals and aspirations with them. This process requires introspection and honesty, a willingness to challenge societal expectations, and an embrace of your unique definition of fulfillment.

It requires recognizing that success isn't a destination, but a journey of continuous growth and learning. There will be setbacks and challenges along the way, these aren't failures, but opportunities for learning and recalibration. Embrace the process, learn from your mistakes, and celebrate your progress, however small. Progress, not perfection, is the hallmark of a successful journey.

This process often involves letting go of the need for external validation. The approval of others shouldn't define success, but your sense of accomplishment and fulfillment. Detaching yourself from the need to compare yourself to others constantly is crucial to cultivating a healthy sense of self-worth.

This shift in perspective is a powerful antidote to feelings of inadequacy and self-doubt. By defining success on your terms, you create a framework for personal growth that is congruent with your values and aspirations. You're no longer striving to meet an arbitrary standard imposed by external forces, you're actively shaping your life to reflect your authentic self.

This is not a passive process. Redefining success requires active effort, consistent self-reflection, and a willingness to challenge ingrained beliefs and societal pressures. It involves constantly evaluating your goals, reassessing your priorities, and making conscious choices that align with your values. It's a process of continuous refinement, a journey of self-discovery that unfolds over time.

The path toward redefining success is deeply personal and unique to each individual. There is no one-size-fits-all formula, and no magic bullet that guarantees instant fulfillment. The process requires introspection, self-awareness, and a willingness to step outside of the constraints of societal expectations.

> *"Success is liking yourself, liking what you do, and liking how you do it."*
>
> May Angelou

Embrace the journey, celebrate your achievements, and never stop learning and growing. Remember, the greatest success is not achieving a predetermined goal, but living a life that is authentically yours, driven by your values, and aligned with your deepest aspirations. Keep moving forward, one step at a time, toward a definition of success that resonates deeply within you. This is where true fulfillment lies, a fulfillment that is far more enduring and meaningful than any external validation could ever provide. The relentless march of life continues, let your authentic self lead the way. The journey itself is a testament to your resilience and the measure of your success. And that, my friends, is a success worth celebrating.

Building Self-Efficacy

Building self-efficacy is the cornerstone of sustained progress. It's the unshakeable belief in your capacity to achieve your goals, overcome obstacles, and navigate the inevitable challenges life throws your way. Without a strong sense of self-efficacy, even the most well-defined goals and meticulously crafted plans can crumble under the weight of doubt and self-criticism. Developing this crucial element is not a passive process, it demands conscious effort, consistent practice, and a willingness to embrace both successes and setbacks as opportunities for growth.

One of the most powerful strategies for building self-efficacy is the deliberate setting of achievable goals. Many individuals falter in their pursuits because they set their sights too high, aiming for grandiose achievements without a roadmap or a realistic understanding of their capabilities. This often results in feelings of overwhelm, frustration, and, ultimately, discouragement. The key lies in breaking down significant, intimidating goals into smaller, more manageable steps.

Imagine, for example, the goal of writing a novel. This task, daunting as it may seem, can be rendered significantly more manageable by breaking it down into smaller, more achievable objectives, such as writing a chapter per week, completing a set number of words daily, or finishing a specific scene before moving on to the next. Each small accomplishment, no matter how seemingly insignificant, contributes to the overall goal and builds a sense of momentum and accomplishment. This incremental progress is not just about efficiency, it's a powerful tool for bolstering self-efficacy. Each small victory reinforces the belief in your capacity to achieve the larger goal.

In the same way, consider the goal of running a marathon. This ambitious undertaking might seem impossible to someone who has never run a mile. However, by starting with shorter runs and gradually increasing distance and intensity, the runner cultivates both physical stamina and psychological resilience. The consistent achievement of these smaller goals, such as completing a 5k, a 10k, and a half-marathon, fosters growing confidence in their ability to conquer the marathon eventually. This phased approach transforms an overwhelming prospect into a series of manageable challenges.

Celebrating these small victories is just as crucial as setting achievable goals. We often overlook the importance of acknowledging and appreciating our accomplishments, focusing instead on what remains to be done. This tendency to minimize our successes undermines our self-efficacy, fostering a sense of inadequacy even when substantial progress has been made. To counteract this, we must consciously cultivate a habit of celebrating our achievements, no matter how small. This could involve anything from a quiet moment of self-reflection to a celebratory dinner with loved ones. The act of acknowledging and appreciating your progress is a powerful affirmation of your capabilities and reinforces your belief in your ability to succeed.

Furthermore, setbacks are inevitable on the path toward achieving any significant goal. They are not failures, but opportunities for learning and growth. Our response to setbacks is critical in shaping our sense of self-efficacy. Individuals with strong self-efficacy tend to view setbacks as temporary challenges rather than permanent defeats. They analyze what went wrong, identify areas for improvement, and adjust their strategies accordingly, rather than allowing setbacks to derail their progress. They learn from their mistakes, adapt their approach, and persevere in the face of adversity. This resilience in the face of adversity is the hallmark of strong self-efficacy.

Developing the ability to learn from setbacks requires a shift in perspective. Instead of viewing mistakes as personal failings, they should be seen as valuable lessons. Analyzing the causes of setbacks, identifying the factors that contributed to the difficulty, and adjusting strategies accordingly are crucial steps in building resilience and bolstering self-efficacy. This process is iterative, it's a continuous cycle of learning, adapting, and persevering. Each setback, when adequately addressed, becomes a stepping stone toward greater success.

Another effective technique for building self-efficacy is to engage in self-affirmation and positive self-talk. This involves consciously replacing negative and self-critical thoughts with positive and empowering statements. Instead of dwelling on failures or focusing on perceived weaknesses, actively focus on your strengths and past successes. Remind yourself of your capabilities and the challenges you've already overcome. Positive self-talk, when practiced consistently, can significantly influence your mindset and boost your self-confidence. It serves as a powerful antidote to self-doubt and reinforces your belief in your ability to succeed.

Visualizing success is also a powerful tool. This involves creating a vivid mental image of yourself achieving your goals. Regularly visualizing success can help to build confidence and motivation. By mentally rehearsing the steps toward success, you are preparing yourself for the challenges ahead and strengthening your belief in your ability to overcome them. The power of visualization lies in its ability to program your subconscious mind for success, making your goals feel more tangible and attainable.

Seeking support from others is another crucial aspect of building self-efficacy. Surrounding yourself with positive and supportive individuals can significantly impact your sense of self-worth and your belief in your capabilities. Sharing your goals and challenges with trusted friends, family, or mentors can provide valuable encouragement and perspective. The support and encouragement from others can significantly reduce feelings of self-doubt and empower you to pursue your goals with renewed confidence.

Furthermore, mastering new skills and acquiring knowledge can also boost your self-efficacy. The process of learning and mastering a new skill not only expands your capabilities, but also reinforces your belief in your capacity to learn and adapt. Each new skill you acquire is a testament to your potential for growth and achievement. This ongoing process of learning and development is essential for maintaining and strengthening your self-efficacy over time.

Finally, remember that building self-efficacy is a continuous process, not a one-time achievement. It requires ongoing self-reflection, consistent effort, and a commitment to continuous learning and growth. There will be ups and downs, successes and setbacks, these are all part of the journey. Embrace the challenges, celebrate the victories, and never lose sight of your goals. By consistently applying these strategies, you will cultivate a strong sense of self-efficacy, empowering you to navigate life's challenges with confidence and resilience, and to keep moving forward, regardless of the obstacles you encounter. The journey is a testament to your strength, and the process of building self-efficacy is a continuous investment in your potential. Embrace the process, celebrate your achievements, large and small, and never stop believing in your ability to succeed. The power lies within you, nurture it and watch it flourish.

Cultivating a Growth Mindset

The journey toward building self-efficacy, as we've explored, is not merely about achieving specific goals, it's about cultivating a fundamental belief in your capacity to learn and grow. This leads us to the crucial concept of a growth mindset. A growth mindset is a robust mental framework that profoundly impacts your ability to overcome limiting beliefs and achieve lasting success. It's the belief that your abilities and intelligence are not fixed, immutable traits, but rather malleable qualities that can be developed and enhanced through dedication, hard work, and a commitment to lifelong learning.

Contrast this with a fixed mindset, where individuals believe their abilities are predetermined and unchangeable. Someone with a fixed mindset might avoid challenges, fearing failure will confirm their perceived limitations. They may interpret setbacks as evidence of inherent inadequacy, leading to discouragement and a reluctance to persevere. They might even compare themselves unfavorably to others, further reinforcing their sense of limitations. This mindset creates a self-fulfilling prophecy, the belief in limitations restricts the very potential it anticipates.

The beauty of a growth mindset lies in its liberating potential. Individuals who embrace this perspective view challenges not as threats, but as opportunities for growth and learning. They see effort as the path to mastery, rather than a sign of weakness. They embrace setbacks not as failures, but as valuable lessons that provide insights into areas needing improvement. And instead of fearing comparison, they see it as an opportunity to learn from others and to strive for continual improvement. This fundamental shift in perspective transforms the entire learning process, making it an engaging and empowering experience.

How does one cultivate this powerful growth mindset? It begins with conscious self-reflection. Identify the areas where you hold a fixed mindset. Are there specific skills or areas of knowledge where you believe your abilities are innate and unchangeable? Recognizing these limiting beliefs is the first step toward dismantling them. This requires honest introspection, a willingness to confront internal narratives that hold you back, and a commitment to challenging your assumptions. Journaling can be an invaluable tool in this process. Regularly recording your thoughts and feelings, examining your responses to challenges, and identifying recurring patterns of negative self-talk can bring to light the underlying beliefs driving your actions.

Once you've identified these limiting beliefs, the next step is to challenge them actively. Ask yourself, what evidence supports this belief? Is there evidence to the contrary? Often, our fixed mindsets are based on past experiences or interpretations of events that may not accurately reflect our true potential. By consciously seeking out counter-evidence, you begin to reshape your perspective. Look to examples of individuals who have overcome significant challenges and achieved extraordinary accomplishments through hard work and persistence. Their stories are powerful reminders that abilities are not fixed, but are cultivated through dedication and effort.

Embrace challenges as opportunities for growth. Step outside your comfort zone. Actively seek out new experiences, even if they feel daunting. The discomfort associated with stretching your abilities is an indicator that you're engaging in meaningful learning. This could involve taking on a new project at work, learning a new skill, or tackling a personal challenge that you've previously avoided. The key is to choose challenges that are appropriately stretching without being overwhelming. Start small, build momentum, and gradually increase the level of difficulty. Remember that progress, not perfection, is the goal.

Cultivating a growth mindset also entails celebrating the process of learning. Focus not just on the outcome, but on the effort and the growth that occur along the way. Acknowledge and appreciate your progress, no matter how small. This means shifting your focus from a purely outcome-based perspective to a process-oriented one. Instead of solely focusing on the ultimate result, concentrate on the journey, acknowledging the milestones along the way, the effort expended, and the lessons learned. These incremental achievements build confidence and reinforce your belief in your ability to grow and improve.

Also, seek feedback and constructive criticism. This is often perceived as threatening by those with a fixed mindset, but it's a critical component of growth. Embrace feedback, even when it's difficult to hear. View it as an opportunity to identify areas for improvement and to learn from your mistakes. This requires developing resilience toward criticism and understanding that it's not a personal attack, but rather a valuable tool for growth. Learn to separate the feedback from your self-worth. Constructive criticism can point out areas where you can learn and grow, and become even better than before.

Remember that the process of cultivating a growth mindset is continuous, it's not a one-time event. It requires consistent effort, self-reflection, and a willingness to embrace the challenges and setbacks that are inherent in the growth process. It's a journey of continual refinement, of constantly questioning your assumptions and seeking out new perspectives. It is also about recognizing that our brains are constantly changing and adapting throughout our lives. This neuroplasticity enables us to learn and develop new skills throughout our lives, regardless of age or background.

The benefits of a growth mindset extend far beyond the attainment of specific goals. It fosters resilience, enhances problem-solving skills, increases creativity, and promotes overall well-being. Individuals with a growth mindset are better equipped to navigate the inevitable challenges of life, adapting to change and learning from their mistakes. They approach life with a sense of optimism and curiosity, viewing setbacks as temporary hurdles rather than permanent limitations. They are more likely to persevere in the face of adversity and to achieve lasting success, not just in their professional lives, but in all aspects of their being.

Embrace the power of lifelong learning. Continuously seek out opportunities to expand your knowledge and develop new skills. This could involve taking courses, reading books, attending workshops, or engaging in self-directed learning projects. The act of learning itself reinforces the growth mindset, reminding you that your abilities are not static, but are capable of continuous development. Embrace the challenges, the frustrations, and the setbacks, for within them lies the potential for remarkable growth and transformation. The path to self-efficacy and lasting success is paved not only with achievement, but also with a constant commitment to growth, a relentless curiosity, and a belief in your limitless potential. This belief is the cornerstone of a life well-lived, a life defined not by limitations, but by the boundless capacity for growth and learning that resides within each of us. Keep moving forward, embracing the journey, and celebrating the continuous growth and evolution of your very being. The power to shape your destiny lies not in what you have already achieved, but in the potential for growth that you consciously nurture and cultivate. That's the real key to unlocking your potential and living a life of purpose and fulfillment.

The Science of Resilience

Building upon the foundation of a growth mindset, we now delve into the fascinating science of resilience, the ability to bounce back from adversity, to adapt to change, and to thrive even in the face of significant challenges. Understanding the science behind resilience empowers us to cultivate this vital trait and navigate life's inevitable storms with greater ease and grace.

Resilience isn't merely about enduring hardship, it's about actively engaging with adversity, learning from it, and emerging stronger on the other side. It's a dynamic process, a continuous interplay between our internal resources and the external challenges we face. It's not a fixed trait, something you either possess or lack, instead, it's a skill that can be developed and strengthened over time.

At its core, resilience is a testament to the remarkable adaptability of the human mind and body. Psychologically, resilient individuals possess a unique blend of characteristics. They tend to have a strong sense of self-efficacy, a belief in their ability to cope with challenges and influence outcomes. This self-belief is intrinsically linked to the growth mindset discussed earlier, it fuels perseverance and helps them overcome setbacks without succumbing to self-doubt.

Furthermore, resilient individuals demonstrate a high degree of optimism and hope. They maintain a positive outlook, even under challenging circumstances, believing that things will eventually improve. This optimistic perspective isn't a naive denial of reality, instead, it's a conscious choice to focus on potential solutions and opportunities for growth. They view challenges as temporary obstacles, not insurmountable barriers.

Crucially, resilient individuals possess strong problem-solving skills. They approach difficulties with a proactive and resourceful mindset, actively seeking solutions rather than passively accepting defeat. They are adept at breaking down complex problems into smaller, manageable steps, developing strategies, and adapting their approach as needed. This strategic thinking is often honed through experience, they learn from past failures, refining their strategies and approaches to future challenges.

Social support plays a vital role in fostering resilience. Strong social connections provide a buffer against stress, offering emotional support, practical assistance, and a sense of belonging. Knowing that they have a network of people to rely on empowers resilient individuals to face their challenges with greater confidence and strength. This network isn't merely about numbers, it's about the quality of relationships, the depth of connection, and the availability of support during times of need.

Beyond the psychological dimensions, resilience also has a physiological component. Chronic stress can wreak havoc on our bodies, increasing the risk of various physical and mental health problems. However, resilient individuals demonstrate a remarkable ability to regulate their stress response. They employ effective coping mechanisms, such as mindfulness, meditation, or physical activity, to manage stress and prevent it from overwhelming them. This regulation helps to mitigate the negative impacts of stress on both their physical and mental well-being.

The scientific understanding of resilience draws heavily upon research in various fields, including psychology, neuroscience, and epidemiology. Numerous studies have explored the factors that contribute to resilience, identifying patterns and common threads among individuals who demonstrate this remarkable capacity. For example, research on the human genome has started to reveal genetic predispositions toward resilience. However, it's crucial to understand that genes are not destiny, environmental factors and personal choices play a crucial role in shaping an individual's resilience. Think of it as a genetic predisposition to build a strong immune system, one that is significantly enhanced through proper nutrition and lifestyle choices.

Research also highlights the critical role of early childhood experiences in shaping resilience. Children who grow up in supportive and nurturing environments, where their emotional needs are met and they feel safe and secure, tend to develop greater resilience. Conversely, children exposed to trauma or adversity may face increased challenges in developing resilience, highlighting the need for early intervention and support.

One particularly insightful area of research focuses on the concept of post-traumatic growth (PTG). This phenomenon describes the positive psychological changes that can occur in the aftermath of trauma or significant adversity. Individuals experiencing PTG often report increased self-awareness, stronger relationships, a greater appreciation for life, and a newfound sense of purpose. This underscores the transformative potential of resilience, it's not just about returning to a pre-trauma state, but about emerging with a deeper understanding of oneself and the world. This growth often comes from the deep introspection and self-discovery that can occur during periods of intense struggle.

The study of resilience also emphasizes the importance of mindfulness and self-compassion. Mindfulness, the practice of paying attention to the present moment without judgment, helps individuals to regulate their emotions and manage stress effectively. Self-compassion, treating oneself with kindness and understanding during times of difficulty, prevents self-criticism from undermining efforts to cope with challenges. These practices are not merely feel-good exercises, they are powerful tools for cultivating resilience and helping individuals to navigate complex emotions and maintain a sense of inner peace.

The neuroscience of resilience offers further insight into the mechanisms involved. Studies using brain imaging techniques have shown that resilient individuals exhibit different patterns of brain activity in response to stress compared to those who are less resilient. Specifically, resilient individuals tend to show greater activation in brain regions associated with emotional regulation and problem-solving, suggesting a greater capacity to manage stressful situations effectively. This doesn't mean that resilient individuals don't experience stress, they possess the skills and resources to manage it more effectively, preventing it from overwhelming their cognitive and emotional capacity.

Building resilience isn't a passive endeavor, it's an active process that requires conscious effort and commitment. It's about cultivating a mindset that embraces challenges, views setbacks as opportunities for growth, and fosters a strong sense of self-belief. This involves developing effective coping mechanisms, building strong social support networks, and practicing self-compassion. It also requires a willingness to learn from past experiences, adapt to changing circumstances, and approach problems with a resourceful and proactive mindset. The journey toward greater resilience is a continuous process of learning, growth, and self-discovery, a testament to the remarkable capacity of the human spirit to overcome adversity and thrive. The more we understand the science behind resilience, the better equipped we are to cultivate this vital quality and navigate life's challenges with greater strength, grace, and inner peace.

In practical terms, strengthening resilience involves actively engaging in activities that build self-efficacy, foster positive emotions, and enhance coping skills. Regular physical exercise has been shown to be highly beneficial, releasing endorphins that improve mood and reduce stress. Mindfulness practices, such as meditation or deep breathing exercises, can also help to regulate the stress response and promote emotional well-being. Engaging in hobbies and activities that bring joy and a sense of accomplishment can enhance self-esteem and provide a welcome distraction from stressors. Seeking professional support, such as therapy or counseling, can be invaluable for individuals struggling to cope with significant adversity. A therapist can provide guidance and support in developing effective coping mechanisms and strategies for managing stress.

Moreover, consciously building and nurturing strong social connections is crucial. Regular interactions with supportive friends, family members, or community groups provide emotional support and a sense of belonging. Joining social clubs, volunteering in the community, or simply engaging in regular social activities can help strengthen these bonds. These connections aren't just comforting during tough times, they act as a protective buffer against stress and promote overall well-being.

Finally, cultivating self-compassion is essential. We must learn to treat ourselves with kindness and understanding, especially during times of difficulty. This means acknowledging our struggles without self-criticism, recognizing that setbacks are a normal part of life, and reminding ourselves that we are not alone in our struggles. Self-compassion allows us to navigate challenges with greater resilience, reducing the negative impact of stress and enhancing our ability to learn and grow from our experiences. Ultimately, building resilience is a continuous journey of self-discovery, adaptation, and growth, a testament to the remarkable capacity of the human spirit to overcome adversity and flourish. It is an ongoing process that requires mindful attention, consistent effort, and an unwavering belief in our potential for growth and transformation.

Developing Coping Mechanisms

Developing effective coping mechanisms is crucial for building resilience. These aren't merely strategies for surviving difficult times; they are tools for thriving, for transforming adversity into opportunities for growth and self-discovery. The ability to effectively manage stress and navigate challenging situations is a cornerstone of resilience, allowing you to not only withstand hardship but also to learn and grow from it. This section will explore a range of practical coping mechanisms, empowering you to develop a personalized toolkit for navigating life's inevitable storms.

One of the most powerful coping mechanisms is **mindfulness**. Mindfulness isn't about escaping reality. It's about engaging with it entirely, without judgment. It's about cultivating an awareness of the present moment—your thoughts, feelings, sensations, and surroundings—without getting carried away by them. When faced with a stressful situation, mindfulness allows you to observe your emotional and physical responses without getting overwhelmed by them. This detached observation can create a sense of calm and clarity, allowing you to respond more effectively.

There are many ways to practice mindfulness. Formal mindfulness meditation involves focusing on your breath, body sensations, or a mantra. However, mindfulness can also be integrated into everyday life. Pay attention to the taste of your food, the feel of the sun on your skin, or the sounds around you. Even a few minutes of mindful attention can make a significant difference in reducing stress and improving your overall sense of well-being. The key is to cultivate a non-judgmental awareness of your experience, accepting whatever arises without trying to change it. Regular practice strengthens this ability, equipping you with a powerful tool for managing stress in challenging situations. Apps like Headspace or Calm offer guided meditations to help you get started.

Closely related to mindfulness is **meditation**, a practice that has been shown to have profound effects on stress reduction and emotional regulation. Meditation involves focusing your attention on a single point of reference, such as your breath, a mantra, or a visual image, for a sustained period. This focused attention helps to quiet the incessant chatter of the mind, reducing feelings of anxiety and promoting a sense of calm and inner peace. Regular meditation practice has been linked to improvements in attention, focus, and emotional regulation, all crucial components of resilience. Various forms of meditation exist, from focused attention meditation to loving-kindness meditation, allowing you to choose a practice that resonates with your personal preferences. Like mindfulness, even short meditation sessions can make a positive impact.

Relaxation techniques are another robust set of coping mechanisms. When faced with stress, our bodies often go into a "fight or flight" response, triggering physiological changes that can be both debilitating and damaging over time. Relaxation techniques help to counteract this response, calming the nervous system and promoting a sense of peace and well-being. Progressive muscle relaxation, for instance, involves systematically tensing and releasing different muscle groups in your body. This process helps to release physical tension, reduce feelings of anxiety, and promote a state of relaxation. Deep breathing exercises, such as diaphragmatic breathing, can also be highly effective. By consciously slowing and deepening your breath, you activate the parasympathetic nervous system, which helps to calm the body and mind.

Beyond physical relaxation techniques, **cognitive restructuring** is a crucial coping mechanism. This involves identifying and challenging negative or unhelpful thought patterns. Often, when faced with adversity, we engage in catastrophic thinking, exaggerating the negative aspects of a situation and minimizing our ability to cope. Cognitive restructuring helps us to identify these negative thought patterns and replace them with more balanced and realistic ones. For example, instead of thinking, "I'll never overcome this," you might reframe the thought to, "This is challenging, but I have overcome difficult situations before, and I can find a way to manage this one too." This process requires self-awareness and practice, but it can significantly improve your ability to cope with stress and build resilience.

Problem-solving skills are essential for managing challenges effectively. This isn't about finding immediate solutions to every problem, but about developing a structured approach to tackling challenges. Effective problem-solving often involves breaking down significant problems into smaller, more manageable steps, identifying potential solutions, evaluating their pros and cons, and selecting the most appropriate course of action. It also includes the ability to adapt your approach as needed, acknowledging that solutions may not always work as planned and may require flexibility and persistence.

Effective problem-solving also hinges on **seeking support**. Resilient individuals understand the value of a strong support network. This might include friends, family, colleagues, mentors, or professional therapists. Sharing your struggles with trusted individuals can provide emotional support, practical assistance, and valuable perspectives. It's important to remember that seeking help is not a sign of weakness, but a sign of strength. It takes courage to acknowledge when we need support, and doing so can significantly enhance our ability to overcome challenges.

In addition to these active coping mechanisms, **self-care** plays a vital role in building resilience. This encompasses a range of activities that promote physical and emotional well-being. Regular exercise, healthy eating, sufficient sleep, and engaging in enjoyable activities all contribute to a stronger sense of self and a greater capacity to cope with stress. Prioritizing self-care is not selfish. It's an essential investment in your well-being and resilience.

Journaling can be a powerful tool for self-reflection and emotional processing. Regularly writing about your thoughts, feelings, and experiences can provide valuable insights into your coping mechanisms, identify patterns of stress, and promote emotional regulation. The act of writing can itself be therapeutic, helping to process emotions and gain perspective.

Humor can also be a surprisingly effective coping mechanism. Finding humor in difficult situations, when appropriate, can help to reduce stress, improve mood, and build resilience. Laughter releases endorphins, which have mood-boosting effects. This is not about minimizing the seriousness of a situation, but about finding moments of levity and perspective.

Finally, remember that **developing coping mechanisms is a journey, not a destination**. It's a continuous process of learning, experimentation, and refinement. What works for one person may not work for another. The key is to explore different strategies, identify those that are most effective for you, and incorporate them into your daily life. Building resilience is a lifelong commitment to self-discovery and growth, empowering you to navigate life's challenges with greater strength, grace, and inner peace. By cultivating these coping mechanisms, you are not merely surviving; you are thriving, transforming adversity into opportunities for personal growth and fulfillment. The journey toward resilience is a testament to the remarkable capacity of the human spirit to overcome challenges and emerge stronger on the other side.

The Importance of Self-Care

In the relentless pursuit of goals and navigating life's inevitable challenges, the importance of self-care often gets overlooked. We push ourselves relentlessly, striving for peak performance and forgetting that our well-being is the foundation upon which all else is built. Building resilience isn't just about developing coping mechanisms for difficult times. It's about proactively nurturing your physical and emotional health, creating a robust system capable of withstanding the inevitable storms. Self-care, far from being a luxury, is an essential pillar of resilience, preventing burnout and enabling you to move forward, even when the going gets tough consistently.

Let's delve deeper into the critical role **self-care** plays in fortifying your resilience. This isn't about indulging in fleeting pleasures. It's about cultivating a mindful and consistent approach to nourishing your body and mind. Consider it an investment in your future self, ensuring you have the energy, focus, and emotional strength to navigate whatever life throws your way.

One of the most fundamental aspects of self-care is adequate sleep. Sleep deprivation significantly impairs cognitive function, reduces emotional regulation, and weakens the immune system, leaving you vulnerable to stress and illness. Aim for 7 to 9 hours of quality sleep each night. Establish a consistent sleep schedule, create a relaxing bedtime routine, and optimize your sleep environment for darkness and quiet. If you struggle with insomnia, consider consulting a healthcare professional to rule out underlying medical conditions and explore strategies for improving sleep hygiene. The impact of sufficient sleep on your resilience cannot be overstated. It's the cornerstone of physical and mental restoration.

Equally crucial is healthy eating. Nourishing your body with a balanced diet provides the fuel your brain and body need to function optimally. Focus on whole, unprocessed foods, including fruits, vegetables, lean proteins, and whole grains. Limit your intake of processed foods, sugary drinks, and excessive caffeine, as these can exacerbate stress and negatively impact your mood. Regular hydration is also essential. Dehydration can lead to fatigue, headaches, and impaired cognitive function, hindering your ability to cope with stress. Pay attention to your body's signals, understanding which foods provide sustained energy and which contribute to energy crashes and mood swings. A well-nourished body is better equipped to handle stress and bounce back from adversity.

Regular physical activity is another essential component of self-care. Exercise isn't just about physical health. It's a powerful tool for stress reduction and emotional regulation. Physical activity releases endorphins, which have mood-boosting effects and help to reduce feelings of anxiety and depression. Find activities you enjoy, whether it's running, swimming, dancing, or yoga. Aim for at least 30 minutes of moderate-intensity exercise most days of the week. Even short bursts of activity throughout the day can make a difference. The key is to find a form of movement that you genuinely enjoy and can incorporate into your routine sustainably. Remember, consistency is key, and finding an activity you love will make it easier to stick with it.

Beyond the physical aspects of self-care, nurturing your emotional well-being is equally important. Engage in activities that bring you joy and relaxation. This could include spending time in nature, listening to music, reading, pursuing hobbies, or spending quality time with loved ones. These activities provide a respite from stress, allowing you to recharge and reconnect with yourself. Prioritize activities that foster a sense of calm, contentment, and connection, reminding yourself of the importance of nurturing your inner world. These activities are not indulgences. They are essential for maintaining emotional balance and building resilience.

Creating a **support network** is also a vital aspect of self-care. Surround yourself with supportive and positive individuals who understand and encourage your journey. Sharing your struggles with trusted friends, family members, or a therapist can provide valuable emotional support and practical assistance. Building strong relationships provides a sense of belonging and reduces feelings of isolation, enhancing your resilience to stress. Remember, seeking support is a sign of strength, not weakness. It takes courage to acknowledge when you need help, and doing so can profoundly impact your ability to overcome challenges.

Learning to set boundaries is another crucial element of self-care. Setting boundaries means protecting your time, energy, and emotional well-being by saying "no" to requests that drain you or conflict with your priorities. This isn't about being selfish, it's about recognizing your limits and prioritizing your well-being. Saying "no" allows you to focus your energy on what truly matters, preventing burnout and fostering a sense of control over your life. Healthy boundaries protect your emotional resources and allow you to dedicate your energy to activities that nurture and support your resilience.

Mindfulness and meditation, as previously discussed, are powerful tools for emotional regulation and stress reduction. Regular practice cultivates self-awareness, enabling you to observe your thoughts and feelings without judgment. This distance allows you to respond more effectively to challenging situations, preventing them from overwhelming you. Even short daily sessions can make a significant difference in your ability to manage stress and maintain emotional equilibrium. Consider incorporating mindfulness into your daily routine, such as during your commute or while enjoying a meal. The cumulative effect of regular mindfulness practice will significantly enhance your resilience.

To effectively integrate self-care into your life, consider creating a weekly self-care plan. This plan should include specific activities that you will engage in each day to promote your physical and emotional well-being. It could include scheduling time for exercise, preparing healthy meals, prioritizing sleep, engaging in relaxing activities, and connecting with supportive individuals. The key is to create a plan that is realistic and sustainable for your lifestyle. By scheduling self-care activities like any other necessary appointment, you prioritize your well-being and make it a non-negotiable part of your routine.

Remember, this is just a template, tailor it to your individual needs and preferences. The most important aspect is to be consistent and prioritize these activities, making them a non-negotiable part of your weekly routine. The beauty of a self-care plan is its adaptability. As your needs change, so too can your plan. Review and adjust your plan regularly to ensure it remains relevant and effective in supporting your well-being. Self-care is not a one-size-fits-all approach, it's a continuous process of self-discovery and adjustment.

By consciously prioritizing self-care, you are not only building resilience but you are investing in your overall well-being and happiness. You are cultivating a lifestyle that allows you to consistently move forward, navigate challenges with greater ease, and thrive in all aspects of your life. Remember, resilience is not simply about surviving adversity; it's about flourishing amidst it, and self-care is the key to unlocking that potential.

Seeking Support and Connection

"No one can Whistle a symphony. It takes a whole orchestra to play it."

H.E. Luccockii

Building resilience isn't a solitary endeavor, it thrives on connection. While self-care forms the bedrock of our inner strength, seeking support and nurturing meaningful relationships are equally crucial pillars in our journey toward adaptability. The strength we derive from our social connections acts as a powerful buffer against life's inevitable storms, providing a safety net and a source of renewed energy when we feel depleted. This isn't about weakness, it's about recognizing the inherent human need for belonging and leveraging the power of community to navigate challenges.

We are, by nature, social creatures. Our brains are wired for connection, we flourish in environments that foster a sense of belonging and mutual support. Isolation, conversely, can be profoundly detrimental to our mental and emotional well-being, increasing our vulnerability to stress and hindering our ability to cope with adversity. This deep-seated need for connection underscores the critical role social support plays in building resilience.

Cultivating a robust support network isn't a passive process, it requires intentionality and effort. It's about consciously building and maintaining relationships with individuals who understand, empathize, and offer genuine support. This doesn't necessarily mean having a large number of acquaintances, quality surpasses quantity in this context. A few close, supportive relationships can provide far more emotional sustenance than a wide circle of superficial contacts.

Identifying those who can offer genuine support is a crucial first step. These are individuals who actively listen without judgment, offering empathy and understanding during challenging times. They are people who celebrate your successes and offer a shoulder to lean on during setbacks. They provide not just emotional support, but also practical assistance when needed, perhaps helping with childcare, offering a helping hand with a task, or simply providing a listening ear. These individuals may include family members, close friends, mentors, colleagues, or members of your faith community.

Maintaining these connections requires effort and consistent nurturing. Just as plants need tending to thrive, relationships require regular attention and care to flourish. This involves making time for meaningful interactions, whether through regular phone calls, video chats, shared activities, or simply spending quality time together. Active listening, expressing appreciation, and offering support in return are essential components of maintaining healthy relationships. Open and honest communication is paramount, sharing both your joys and your struggles builds trust and strengthens the bonds of connection.

However, building a support network isn't just about maintaining existing relationships, it also involves actively seeking out new connections. This can be achieved through joining groups or organizations aligned with your interests or values, engaging in volunteer work, or simply striking up conversations with people you encounter in your daily life. Participating in activities that foster social interaction, such as joining a sports team, taking a class, or attending community events, provides opportunities to forge new friendships and expand your support network.

Sometimes, seeking professional support becomes necessary. This isn't a sign of weakness, it's a demonstration of self-awareness and a proactive approach to managing mental and emotional well-being. Therapists, counselors, and other mental health professionals provide a safe and confidential space to explore challenges, develop coping strategies, and gain valuable insights into your emotional landscape. They offer a structured framework for processing difficult experiences and building skills for navigating future adversity. Remember, accessing professional help is a sign of strength and a commitment to self-care. It's an act of self-preservation, investing in your long-term well-being and resilience.

Furthermore, recognizing your limitations and acknowledging when you need help is vital. Many individuals struggle with asking for support, believing it represents a personal failing. This couldn't be further from the truth. Seeking help demonstrates courage, self-awareness, and a commitment to your well-being. It's an acknowledgment that you don't have to face life's challenges alone, and that accepting support from others doesn't diminish your strength, it amplifies it.

Once you've identified your support system, learn to articulate your needs effectively. This involves clearly and concisely communicating your challenges and what kind of support you require. Avoid vague or indirect requests, be specific about what you need from your support network. For instance, instead of saying, "I'm feeling overwhelmed," try saying, "I'm feeling overwhelmed with work and could really use some help with childcare this week. Would you be able to watch the kids on Tuesday evening?"

Remember, the effectiveness of your support system hinges on reciprocal support. While receiving support is crucial, it's equally important to offer support to others within your network. This creates a sense of mutual obligation and strengthens the bonds of connection. By providing support to others, you not only deepen your relationships, but also experience the positive emotional effects of giving back, creating a virtuous cycle of connection and support. This reciprocity reinforces the foundation of your network, making it even more resilient in times of hardship.

Beyond immediate social connections, exploring broader communities can enrich your support system. Online communities, support groups focused on specific challenges, and faith-based organizations can provide a sense of belonging and connection with like-minded individuals. These communities offer valuable insights, shared experiences, and a sense of solidarity, reminding you that you are not alone in your struggles. Online support groups, in particular, offer anonymity and accessibility, allowing individuals to connect with others who share similar experiences from the comfort of their own homes.

Building and maintaining a strong support network is an ongoing process. Relationships evolve, and your needs may change over time. Regularly assess your support system, identify any gaps, and actively work to cultivate new connections or strengthen existing ones. Be open to new relationships and opportunities to expand your network. It's a continual journey, and the effort you invest will significantly enhance your resilience and your ability to thrive amidst life's uncertainties. Remember, your support network isn't a static entity, it's a dynamic ecosystem that requires consistent cultivation and nurturing to remain robust and effective in supporting your journey. Investing in your relationships is an investment in your resilience. Nurture those connections, and you will reap the rewards in times of both challenge and triumph.

Adapting to Change

> *"The measure of intelligence is the ability to change."*
>
> Albert Einstein

Adapting to change is not merely about surviving, it's about thriving amidst the inevitable shifts life throws our way. It's a skill honed through conscious effort and a mindset that embraces the unknown. The ability to adapt is not an innate trait reserved for a select few, it's a capacity we all possess, waiting to be cultivated and strengthened. This process begins with recognizing that change is a constant, an inherent aspect of human experience. Resistance to change only exacerbates its impact, while acceptance and proactive adaptation pave the way for resilience and growth.

One of the most significant hurdles in adapting to change lies in our tendency to cling to the familiar. We develop routines, habits, and comfort zones that provide a sense of security and predictability. However, when faced with unexpected changes, these ingrained patterns can become obstacles, hindering our ability to adjust and move forward. The first step in effectively navigating change, therefore, is embracing flexibility, a willingness to deviate from established routines and explore new possibilities.

This doesn't imply a chaotic abandonment of structure, instead, it's about cultivating a mindset that allows for fluidity and adaptability. It's about understanding that life's path is rarely linear and that unexpected detours are not necessarily setbacks, but opportunities for growth and discovery. Consider the example of an individual whose career path takes an unexpected turn. A layoff forces a reevaluation of professional goals, leading to the exploration of a new field that ultimately proves more fulfilling. The initial shock and uncertainty are undeniable, but by embracing flexibility and exploring alternative avenues, the individual discovers a more aligned and potentially rewarding career trajectory.

Flexibility extends beyond professional life, it permeates all aspects of our existence. Consider a family facing a relocation to a new city. The disruption to established routines, the loss of familiar surroundings, and the challenges of building a new social network can be overwhelming. However, a flexible approach, embracing the opportunity to explore new communities, discover hidden gems in the new city, and forge new connections, can transform what might have been a traumatic experience into a catalyst for growth and connection. This flexible approach allows them not just to adjust, but to create a new life filled with possibilities.

Viewing change as an opportunity rather than a threat is paramount to effective adaptation. This shift in perspective requires a conscious effort to reframe our thinking. Instead of focusing on what's been lost or disrupted, we need to train our minds to search for the potential benefits and positive aspects of change. This positive reframing can significantly reduce stress and anxiety, fostering a sense of empowerment and control. For example, an unexpected illness might lead to a re-evaluation of lifestyle choices, emphasizing healthy habits and a deeper appreciation for physical and mental well-being.

Developing strategies for managing uncertainty is crucial. Uncertainty is an inherent companion to change, generating anxiety and fear. However, we can mitigate this discomfort by establishing coping mechanisms and strategies. Planning and preparation, even in the face of the unknown, can create a sense of control and reduce anxiety. Creating a detailed plan and breaking down significant changes into smaller, manageable steps can make the process less daunting and more manageable. Setting realistic expectations and celebrating small victories along the way can reinforce a sense of progress and maintain momentum.

Moreover, mindfulness practices, such as meditation and deep breathing exercises, can be invaluable tools for managing the stress and uncertainty associated with change. These techniques help to calm the nervous system, improve focus, and enhance emotional regulation. Regular practice can build resilience and improve the ability to respond to unexpected events with greater composure and adaptability. The ability to observe thoughts and feelings without judgment allows us to manage the emotional rollercoaster of change with greater awareness and acceptance.

Another powerful approach to adapting to change involves learning from previous experiences. Reflecting on past challenges and how we successfully navigated them offers valuable insights and builds confidence for future transitions. Identifying patterns in our responses to change can help us develop more effective strategies for managing future disruptions. What coping mechanisms have proven successful in the past? What could we have done differently? Asking these questions fosters self-awareness and promotes growth, making us better equipped to handle future changes.

Seeking support from others is another essential element in successfully navigating change. Talking to trusted friends, family members, mentors, or therapists can provide emotional support, guidance, and a fresh perspective. Sharing our experiences and concerns can lessen the burden and offer new ways of understanding and responding to challenges. A supportive network can offer encouragement, practical assistance, and valuable insights, boosting resilience and fostering a sense of community during times of transition.

Finally, remember to celebrate your progress. Adapting to change is a journey, not a destination. Acknowledging and celebrating even small victories along the way reinforces a sense of accomplishment, motivates continued effort, and builds self-confidence. This positive reinforcement helps to maintain momentum and counter the potential for discouragement during challenging periods.

Celebrating the milestones, no matter how small, reinforces the fact that you are progressing and capable of adapting to the changes in your life.

In conclusion, adapting to change is a lifelong process that requires conscious effort, flexibility, and a positive mindset. By embracing uncertainty, viewing change as an opportunity for growth, developing coping strategies, and seeking support, we can build resilience and navigate life's inevitable transitions with greater ease and confidence. It's not about avoiding change, but about mastering our response to it, transforming challenges into opportunities for personal growth, and creating a life of resilience and adaptability. Remember, the capacity for adaptation is inherent within each of us, it's a skill waiting to be honed and strengthened, enabling us to thrive amidst life's ever-changing currents. Embrace the journey, celebrate the small victories, and never underestimate your capacity to adapt and overcome. The power to adapt resides within you.

SMART Goal Setting

"A goal without a plan is just a wish"

Antoine de Saint-Exupéry

Having established the importance of adaptability and a forward-looking mindset, we now turn to a crucial tool for navigating change and achieving lasting personal growth: goal setting. While simply deciding to "move forward" is a decisive first step, without a clear direction, momentum can quickly dissipate. This is where the power of SMART goals comes into play. SMART goals are not just about setting aspirations, they're about creating a roadmap for achieving them, a pathway that breaks down overwhelming objectives into manageable steps, fostering a sense of accomplishment and maintaining momentum even during challenging periods.

The acronym SMART stands for Specific, Measurable, Achievable, Relevant, and Time-bound. Let's explore each element in detail. A **Specific** goal leaves no room for ambiguity. Instead of saying, "I want to be healthier," a specific goal might be, "I will walk for 30 minutes three times a week." Notice the precision, there's no room for interpretation. Similarly, a vague goal like "I want to improve my finances" becomes specific when reframed as "I will save $500 by the end of the year by reducing my monthly dining-out expenses by $100." Specificity provides clarity and direction, making the goal easier to pursue.

Measurable goals allow you to track your progress and stay motivated. How will you know if you're succeeding? With measurable goals, the answer is clear. For the fitness goal, you can track your walks using a fitness tracker or mark them off on a calendar. For the financial goal, you can monitor your spending and savings regularly using a budgeting app or spreadsheet. The ability to quantify progress provides a tangible sense of accomplishment, fueling further effort. Without measurability, your goals remain abstract, making it difficult to gauge your success.

Achievable goals are realistic and attainable, given your current circumstances and resources. While ambition is essential, setting unattainable goals can lead to discouragement and frustration. Consider your current capabilities and limitations. If you haven't exercised regularly in years, aiming to run a marathon in three months is likely unrealistic and potentially harmful. A more achievable goal might be to walk briskly for 30 minutes three times a week for the first month, gradually increasing the duration and intensity. Start small, build momentum, and progressively challenge yourself as your capabilities grow.

The **Relevance** of a goal hinges on its alignment with your broader life goals and values. Is this goal fundamental to you, or is it something you're pursuing because someone else suggested it? If a goal doesn't resonate with your core values and aspirations, it's unlikely you'll maintain the motivation to see it through. Consider your long-term objectives, how does this goal contribute to your overall well-being and sense of purpose? Ensure your goals are genuinely meaningful to you, not just another item on a checklist. A goal lacking relevance will often be abandoned before completion.

Finally, a **Time-bound** goal has a clear deadline. This creates a sense of urgency and helps prevent procrastination. The time frame should be realistic and challenging, not overwhelming. Setting deadlines for smaller milestones within a larger goal can further enhance motivation and track progress effectively. Having a clear endpoint for each step of your journey provides a sense of closure and achievement, spurring you on to the next stage. Without deadlines, goals can linger indefinitely, diminishing their impact.

Let's illustrate the application of SMART goals with several examples across different life areas:

Career: Instead of "Get a better job," a SMART goal would be: "Obtain a promotion to Senior Marketing Manager by December 31st, 2025, by completing the required training courses and exceeding performance expectations in my current role, as evidenced by positive performance reviews and increased sales figures." This goal is specific, measurable (performance reviews, sales figures), achievable (defined steps), relevant (career advancement), and time-bound (December 31st, 2025).

Health & Fitness: Instead of "Lose weight," a SMART goal might be:"Lose 10 pounds by June 1st, 2025, by following a balanced diet plan, incorporating 30 minutes of exercise five times a week, and tracking my progress using a fitness tracker and a food diary." This goal is specific, measurable (weight loss, exercise frequency, food intake), achievable (realistic weight loss goal and exercise plan), relevant (improved health and well-being), and time-bound (June 1st, 2025).

Personal Development: Instead of "Learn a new language," a SMART goal would be: "Achieve a conversational level of fluency in Spanish by December 31st, 2025, by attending a language class twice a week, completing online language learning modules daily, and engaging in conversational practice with native speakers at least once a week." This goal is specific, measurable (conversational fluency, class attendance, module completion, practice sessions), achievable (defined learning plan), relevant (personal enrichment), and time-bound (December 31st, 2025).

Relationships: Instead of "Improve my communication with my partner," a SMART goal could be: "Have a constructive and open conversation with my partner about our communication style at least twice a month, starting this month, focusing on active listening and expressing emotions clearly. We will use the Gottman Method tools we learned in our relationship therapy sessions to navigate our discussions constructively." This goal is specific (conversation frequency, focus areas, specific tools), measurable (frequency of conversations, use of specific methods), achievable (assuming willingness from both partners and available resources), relevant (stronger relationship), and time-bound (ongoing with a defined monthly frequency).

Financial: Instead of "Save money," a SMART goal might be: "Save $5,000 by December 31st, 2025, by automating monthly transfers of $400 into a high-yield savings account, tracking my spending, and reducing non-essential expenses by 10% using a budgeting app." This goal is specific, measurable (savings amount, monthly transfers, spending reduction), achievable (realistic savings target and budget plan), relevant (financial security), and time-bound (December 31st, 2025).

Remember, these are just examples. The key is to personalize your goals according to your unique circumstances and aspirations. The process of defining SMART goals is a powerful exercise in self-reflection and clarity. It pushes you to confront your dreams, define your direction, and create a realistic framework for achieving lasting positive change.

To help you in this process, I've included a goal-setting worksheet at the end of this chapter. This worksheet will guide you through each element of the SMART framework, helping you transform vague aspirations into concrete, actionable goals. Use it as a tool for self-reflection and planning, let it be your companion as you embark on your journey of continuous growth and achievement. Don't be afraid to revise your goals as your circumstances change. The important thing is to keep moving forward, one step at a time. The power to shape your future lies in your hands, use the SMART goal-setting framework as a compass to guide you toward a life filled with purpose and accomplishment. Remember, consistent effort, even in small increments, is the cornerstone of lasting success. The journey may have its challenges, but the rewards of achieving your SMART goals will far outweigh any temporary setbacks. Embrace the process, celebrate your milestones, and never underestimate your potential for growth and transformation. The path to a fulfilling life is paved with well-defined, achievable goals.

Breaking Down Large Goals

"You do not rise to the level of your goals. You fall to the level of your systems."

James Clear, author of Atomic Habits

Having laid the foundation for setting SMART goals, we now address a critical aspect of achieving them, particularly when faced with seemingly insurmountable objectives: breaking down significant goals into smaller, more manageable steps. Many individuals falter not due to a lack of ambition, but because they are overwhelmed by the sheer magnitude of their aspirations. The prospect of achieving a significant life change, such as writing a novel, learning a new language fluently, starting a business, or significantly improving one's physical fitness, can feel daunting, even paralyzing. The key to overcoming this inertia lies in strategically dismantling these significant goals into a series of smaller, achievable milestones. This approach fosters a sense of consistent progress, preventing discouragement and maintaining momentum.

The human brain thrives on immediate gratification. It is wired to respond favorably to quick wins and readily visible progress. When faced with a significant, long-term goal, the lack of immediate results can be disheartening. This is where breaking down the goal is crucial. By dividing your objective into smaller, more readily attainable steps, you create a system of regular accomplishments, each one feeding into the larger goal. Each small victory boosts your confidence, motivation, and overall sense of self-efficacy, propelling you toward the ultimate objective.

Consider the analogy of climbing a mountain. Looking at the towering peak from the base can be intimidating, the distance appears insurmountable. However, if you focus on reaching the next landmark, a rocky outcrop, a patch of relatively level ground, or a bend in the trail, the journey becomes less daunting. Each step, each milestone, brings you closer to the summit, providing a sense of accomplishment and reinforcing your determination. Similarly, breaking down significant goals provides a roadmap, a clear path with easily identifiable checkpoints.

1. I want to go ahead and outline a step-by-step approach to breaking down the understanding of the outcome you want. This requires careful introspection. What is the specific, measurable, achievable, relevant, and time-bound (SMART) goal you are striving for? Please write it down. Be explicit. Leave no room for ambiguity. This detailed articulation will serve as your guiding star throughout the entire process. For example, if your goal is to write a novel, define the genre, target word count, and intended publication method.

2. **Identify Key Milestones:** Once your overarching goal is clearly defined, identify the key milestones or checkpoints that must be reached to achieve it. These are significant markers of progress signifying substantial movement toward your objective. In the case of writing a novel, key milestones could include completing the outline, finishing the first draft, completing the editing process, and securing representation from a literary agent. These are not daily tasks. Instead, they are more considerable achievements that mark meaningful progress.

3. **Break Down Milestones into Smaller Tasks:** Now, focus on each milestone individually. Could you break it down into smaller, more manageable tasks? These tasks should be specific, achievable within a short timeframe, and easily trackable. For the "completing the outline" milestone,

individual tasks might involve brainstorming ideas, outlining each chapter, drafting the character profiles, or creating a timeline of events.

4. **Set Realistic Timelines:** Assign realistic deadlines to each minor task and milestone. You can avoid overly ambitious scheduling, as it can lead to frustration and a loss of momentum. It's better to slightly underestimate the time required to complete each step to avoid burnout. Consider any potential obstacles that might delay your progress.

5. **Track Your Progress:** Create a system to monitor your progress. Use a calendar, a spreadsheet, a project management app, or even a simple checklist. I believe regularly reviewing your progress is crucial to maintaining motivation and identifying potential challenges that may require adjustments to your plan.

6. **Embrace Flexibility and Adaptability:** It is unlikely that your initial plan will remain utterly unchanged throughout the entire process. Life is full of unexpected twists and turns. Be prepared to adapt your approach, adjust timelines, and even modify smaller tasks as needed. The key is to remain flexible and focused on the overarching goal while making necessary adjustments.

7. **Celebrate Milestones:** Each time you achieve a milestone, take time to celebrate your accomplishments. Acknowledge your progress. Reward yourself. This reinforcement positively affects your motivation and encourages persistence. A small celebration can be as simple as enjoying a favorite meal or taking a relaxing bath.

Let's apply this framework to the example of running a marathon. The ultimate goal: Complete a marathon.

Key Milestones: Complete a 5M, 10M, and half-marathon. Build up stamina to run for extended durations without significant pain or discomfort.

Learn proper running techniques to minimize the risk of injury. Develop a comprehensive training plan.

Smaller Tasks: Gradually increase running distance weekly, incorporate interval training, follow a structured running plan, find a good running group, choose the right running shoes, and ensure adequate nutrition and hydration.

Now, consider learning a new language fluently.

Key Milestones: Learn the alphabet and basic pronunciation. Achieve basic conversational skills in daily situations. Read simple texts and understand basic grammar. Achieve fluency in speaking, reading, and writing.

Smaller Tasks: Study vocabulary words daily, learn grammar rules in increments, practice speaking with native speakers, immerse oneself in the language through movies, music, and books, utilize language learning apps, and attend language exchange meetings.

Starting a business can be equally daunting, but it can be broken down into more manageable steps.

Key Milestones: Develop a business plan, secure funding, establish a legal structure, build a website or physical store, create marketing materials, establish a customer base, etc.

Smaller Tasks: Research market competition, identify target audience, create a product or service offering, develop marketing strategies, establish partnerships, manage daily operations, etc.

The consistent application of this strategy, breaking down significant, overwhelming goals into a series of smaller, achievable steps, is the cornerstone of maintaining momentum and achieving lasting success. It encourages a sense of accomplishment, reduces feelings of being overwhelmed, and provides a path to navigate challenges with clarity and purpose. Remember, consistent effort, even in small increments, is the foundation of meaningful progress. Embrace the journey, celebrate your milestones, and never underestimate your potential for growth and transformation. The path to a fulfilling life is paved with well-defined, achievable steps, meticulously planned and consistently executed.

Overcoming Procrastination

Procrastination: A Thief of Time and Dreams

We've established the importance of breaking down significant goals into smaller, manageable steps. However, even with a well-defined roadmap, many individuals still struggle to maintain momentum. A significant hurdle that frequently derails progress is procrastination. It is the silent saboteur that whispers doubts and excuses, preventing us from taking even the most minor steps forward. Understanding and overcoming procrastination is, therefore, crucial for achieving our goals and realizing our full potential.

Procrastination isn't simply laziness, it is a complex behavioral pattern often rooted in deeper psychological factors. Fear of failure, perfectionism, a lack of clarity regarding the task at hand, or simply feeling overwhelmed are common culprits. The task itself might seem too daunting, leading to a paralysis of inaction. This feeling is amplified when the task is vaguely defined, lacks clear instructions, or is perceived as incredibly time-consuming. The brain, seeking immediate gratification, opts for easier, more immediately rewarding activities, postponing the challenging task indefinitely.

I want you to know that understanding the root cause of your procrastination is the first step toward overcoming it. Journaling can be incredibly insightful. Take some time to honestly reflect on why you procrastinate. Are you afraid of failure? Do you fear success? Are you overwhelmed by the scope of the task? Identifying the underlying cause empowers you to address it directly. For example, if fear of failure is the primary driver, you can focus on developing a more positive self-image and building resilience to setbacks. If the task feels overwhelming, break it down into even smaller, more digestible pieces.

Time management techniques are essential tools in the fight against procrastination. Many methods exist, and finding the one that best suits your personality and work style is key. The Pomodoro Technique, for example, involves working in focused bursts of 25 minutes followed by a 5-minute break. This structured approach helps maintain concentration and prevents burnout. After four Pomodoros, a more extended break of 15 to 20 minutes is recommended. This method provides a sense of accomplishment with each completed Pomodoro, combating the inertia of an enormous, looming task.

Another effective strategy is the Eisenhower Matrix, also known as the Urgent-Important Matrix. This method categorizes tasks based on urgency and importance. By prioritizing tasks using this framework, you can focus your energy on the most crucial activities, avoiding the trap of spending time on less critical tasks. This method is particularly useful in managing multiple tasks simultaneously, helping to prevent procrastination by ensuring that time is allocated effectively.

Furthermore, creating a detailed schedule can significantly reduce procrastination. Allocate specific time slots for particular tasks in your daily or weekly planner. This pre-emptive scheduling commits you to completing the tasks during those designated times. It transforms the vague notion of "I'll do it later" into a concrete commitment. Treat these scheduled time blocks as non-negotiable appointments, as important as a meeting with your boss or a doctor's appointment. By consistently adhering to your schedule, you build discipline and create a habit of completing tasks on time.

Beyond structured techniques, cultivating self-compassion is essential. Be kind to yourself. Everyone procrastinates sometimes. Instead of berating yourself for past procrastination, acknowledge it, understand its underlying cause, and move forward with a renewed commitment to overcome it. Self-criticism is a significant barrier to progress, self-compassion is its antidote.

Remember that setbacks are a natural part of the process, they don't define your abilities or potential.

Another critical element is minimizing distractions. Identify your biggest time-wasters: social media, email, unnecessary meetings, or even simply excessive phone calls. Consciously limit exposure to these distractions during your focused work periods. Turn off notifications, put your phone on silent, close unnecessary browser tabs, and create a distraction-free workspace. The more you minimize external disruptions, the more focused and productive you can be, reducing the likelihood of procrastination.

Breaking down large tasks into smaller, more manageable components is a core principle we've discussed. But this needs to be refined. If a task still feels too daunting even after being broken down, break it down further. Reduce the scope to its most basic elements. Instead of "write a chapter," focus on "write 500 words." Instead of "cleaning the entire house," focus on "cleaning the kitchen." These micro-tasks are more straightforward to start, fostering a sense of accomplishment that fuels further progress.

Gamification can also play a crucial role in combating procrastination. Turn your tasks into a game. Use reward systems, progress bars, or checklists to track your progress and celebrate accomplishments. Reward yourself for completing even small tasks, this positive reinforcement strengthens your commitment and encourages you to continue. This motivational approach transforms a mundane task into an engaging challenge.

Finally, don't hesitate to ask for support. Enlist the help of friends, family, colleagues, or mentors. Sharing your goals and challenges with others can provide accountability and motivation. A supportive network can offer encouragement and practical advice, helping you avoid falling back into patterns of procrastination. A structured accountability group, where individuals commit to working on their goals together and report their progress regularly, can be especially effective.

In conclusion, procrastination is a common obstacle on the path to achieving our goals. It is not a character flaw, but rather a behavior that can be understood and overcome with conscious effort and the right strategies. By understanding the underlying causes, employing effective time management techniques, cultivating self-compassion, and creating a supportive environment, you can conquer procrastination and unlock your full potential. The path to success is paved with consistent effort, even in small increments. Embrace the journey, celebrate your progress, and never underestimate your capacity for resilience and growth. Remember, the small steps you take consistently, even when faced with inertia and the urge to procrastinate, are what truly define your achievement and fulfillment. The power to overcome procrastination lies within you, unleash it and move forward.

Building Habits for Success

"We are what we repeatedly do. Excellence, then, is not an act, but a habit."

Will Durant, Summarizing Aristotle

Building a life of consistent achievement hinges on more than just setting goals, it necessitates the cultivation of supportive habits. Think of habits as the invisible scaffolding that holds up your ambitions. Without a strong foundation of good habits, even the most meticulously crafted goals can crumble under the weight of procrastination, distractions, and inconsistent effort. This section explores the crucial role habit-building plays in maintaining momentum and achieving lasting success.

The power of habit lies in its automaticity. Once a habit is ingrained, it requires minimal conscious effort. This frees up mental energy and allows us to focus on more complex tasks and challenges, essentially putting our goals on autopilot. The seemingly mundane routines of brushing your teeth, making your bed, and preparing a healthy breakfast are all examples of habits that, while small, contribute to a sense of order and control in your daily life. Extending this principle to larger goals, building positive habits becomes the key to consistent progress.

The process of habit formation isn't about sudden, dramatic transformations, it's a gradual, iterative process. Neuroscientists have shown that new neural pathways are created in the brain each time we repeat a behavior. The more consistently we engage in a particular behavior, the stronger this neural pathway becomes, making the behavior increasingly automatic and easier to perform. This is why consistent effort is so vital. Don't expect immediate, perfect results, embrace the journey and celebrate incremental improvements.

One highly effective framework for habit building is the "habit loop," which consists of three key components: the cue, the routine, and the reward. The cue is the trigger that initiates the behavior. It could be a specific time of day, a location, a feeling, or even another habit. The routine is the actual behavior you want to establish. This could be anything from daily exercise to studying for an hour each evening. The reward is the positive reinforcement that strengthens the connection between the cue and the routine. This reward could be anything that provides a sense of satisfaction or accomplishment.

Let's consider an example. Suppose you want to establish the habit of daily meditation. Your cue could be setting an alarm on your phone at 7 a.m. each morning. The routine is the act of meditation itself, a 10-minute session using a guided meditation app. The reward could be the sense of calmness and clarity you experience after the session, or a cup of herbal tea you enjoy immediately afterward. By consistently pairing the cue, routine, and reward, you reinforce the neural pathway associated with the desired behavior, making it more likely to occur in the future.

Another powerful technique is habit stacking, where you link a new habit to an existing one. If you already have the habit of brushing your teeth every morning, you could stack a new habit onto it, such as drinking a glass of water or doing some quick stretches immediately after brushing. This leverages an already established habit to anchor a new one, making it easier to incorporate into your routine. The existing habit acts as a reliable cue for the new one.

It's also essential to understand the concept of "habit inertia." This refers to the tendency for habits to persist, even if they are no longer serving you well. Breaking bad habits is often more challenging than building new ones because they are deeply ingrained in your neural pathways. However, by understanding the habit loop, you can strategically dismantle unhealthy habits by identifying and altering the cue, routine, or reward. You could replace a mindless snacking habit with a healthier alternative, or replace late-night screen time with a relaxing bedtime routine.

The key to success in habit formation lies in consistency and patience. Don't get discouraged if you miss a day or two. View setbacks as opportunities for learning and adjustment. The most important thing is to get back on track as quickly as possible and continue building the habit. Be kind to yourself, progress is not linear.

Let's explore some specific examples of habits that are strongly correlated with success. Daily exercise, for instance, not only improves physical health but also enhances mental clarity, energy levels, and overall mood. Regular physical activity reduces stress, improves sleep quality, and fosters resilience, all crucial factors contributing to the ability to navigate challenges and maintain momentum toward goals.

Mindfulness practices, such as meditation or yoga, are equally important. These practices help to cultivate self-awareness, reduce stress, and improve focus. They train your mind to be present in the moment rather than dwelling on past regrets or future anxieties. This heightened self-awareness allows you to recognize and address unproductive behaviors or thought patterns that hinder progress.

Consistent work on personal projects, whether it's writing, painting, coding, or any other pursuit you are passionate about, fosters discipline and resilience. It teaches you to persevere in the face of setbacks, to overcome obstacles, and to celebrate even small victories. This dedication to personal projects builds confidence and cultivates a growth mindset, enhancing your ability to approach challenges with determination and optimism.

Cultivating a gratitude practice is another habit with significant benefits. By regularly taking time to reflect on things you are grateful for, you shift your focus from what is lacking to what is abundant in your life. This positive shift in perspective fosters resilience, reduces stress, and enhances overall well-being. A gratitude journal, for example, can serve as a powerful tool for cultivating this habit.

Strategic planning and review are also critical habits for success. Regularly reviewing your progress toward your goals allows you to identify what is working well and what needs adjustments. It prevents you from getting sidetracked and keeps you focused on your long-term objectives. This regular evaluation process fosters adaptability and strengthens your ability to remain on course.

Effective time management is another essential habit to cultivate. Learning to prioritize tasks, schedule your time effectively, and eliminate time-wasting activities frees up mental energy and reduces stress. This efficiency allows you to dedicate more time and focus to activities that directly contribute to your goals. Techniques like the Pomodoro Technique or time blocking can be beneficial in this regard.

Finally, building and maintaining strong social connections is vital. Surrounding yourself with supportive, positive individuals fosters resilience and motivation. These relationships provide a sense of belonging, encouragement, and accountability, all crucial elements in maintaining momentum during challenging times. Investing time in meaningful relationships provides a crucial emotional buffer, enhancing your ability to cope with stress and setbacks.

Building positive habits is not a quick fix, it is a continuous process that requires consistent effort, patience, and self-compassion. However, the rewards are immeasurable. By cultivating these habits, you create a foundation for lasting success, transforming your approach to goal attainment from a series of sporadic bursts of effort to a consistent, sustainable journey of growth and achievement. Remember, the journey of a thousand miles begins with a single step, and the consistent repetition of those steps, guided by positive habits, will ultimately lead you to your destination. Embrace the process, celebrate your progress, and never underestimate the transformative power of consistent action.

Maintaining Motivation

Maintaining motivation is the lifeblood of achieving any worthwhile goal. It is the internal engine that keeps you moving forward, even when the road gets bumpy and the destination seems far off. While setting clear, achievable goals provides direction, maintaining motivation provides the fuel for the journey. This isn't about some fleeting burst of enthusiasm, it is about cultivating a sustainable mindset that allows you to consistently put in the work, even when faced with inevitable setbacks and challenges.

One of the most critical aspects of maintaining motivation is consistent self-reflection. Please check in with yourself to see your progress, identify potential roadblocks, and adjust your strategies as needed. This isn't about self-criticism, it is about honest self-assessment. Ask yourself: Am I still on track with my goals? What obstacles am I encountering? What adjustments can I make to overcome these challenges? What aspects of this process are bringing me joy and fulfillment, and what parts are draining my energy? Honest answers to these questions provide invaluable insights into your progress and allow you to adapt your approach accordingly.

A powerful tool for self-reflection is journaling. Regular journaling allows you to track your progress, document your feelings, and identify patterns in your thinking and behavior. Consider dedicating a few minutes each day or week to writing about your experiences, challenges, and successes. This process of putting your thoughts and feelings into words can provide surprising clarity and help you identify areas where you might need to make adjustments. You don't need to worry about writing perfectly, the goal is to express yourself honestly and openly. This self-reflective practice will enhance your self-awareness and help you understand your motivational patterns.

Celebrating achievements, both big and small, is another crucial component of maintaining motivation. We often focus on the end goal, overlooking the many smaller victories along the way. Acknowledging and celebrating these smaller wins helps to keep your spirits high and reinforces the positive feelings associated with your progress. This could be anything from completing a specific task to reaching a milestone. Find ways to reward yourself for your efforts, whether it is a small treat, a relaxing activity, or simply taking some time to acknowledge your accomplishments. This positive reinforcement strengthens your commitment to your goals and makes the journey more enjoyable.

A common pitfall is falling into the trap of comparing yourself to others. Social media, in particular, can create a distorted perception of reality, leading to feelings of inadequacy and discouragement. Remember that everyone's journey is unique. Focus on your progress rather than comparing yourself to others. Celebrate your achievements and learn from your setbacks without judging yourself against the perceived successes of others. Your journey is your own, and it is perfectly valid to celebrate your unique milestones at your own pace.

Adjusting your strategies is a sign of strength, not weakness. As you progress toward your goals, you may discover that your initial plan needs adjustments. Be flexible and adaptable, and don't be afraid to change course if necessary. This might involve re-evaluating your goals, adjusting your timeline, or seeking guidance from others. This flexibility is key to staying motivated and overcoming obstacles. Rigidity in your approach can often lead to frustration and, ultimately, demotivation.

Burnout is a real threat when pursuing ambitious goals. It is crucial to recognize the signs of burnout, such as exhaustion, cynicism, and reduced professional efficacy, and to take proactive steps to prevent it. Burnout is not a sign of weakness, it is a sign that you need to make some adjustments to your approach. This could involve taking breaks, re-evaluating your workload, seeking support from others, or prioritizing self-care. Burnout is not just about physical exhaustion, it is also about mental and emotional depletion. Prioritizing rest is just as important as the work itself.

Maintaining enthusiasm is critical. This means finding ways to keep your passion alive throughout the process. One way to do this is to regularly remind yourself of why you set the goal in the first place. Connect with the deeper reasons behind your ambitions, your values, your aspirations, and your long-term vision. This reconnection to the "why" can re-ignite your passion and help you push through challenging times.

Another technique is to break down significant goals into smaller, more manageable steps. This creates a sense of accomplishment with each completed step, which keeps you motivated and moving forward. This prevents the feeling of being overwhelmed by the magnitude of the overall goal. Small, consistent progress reinforces your sense of capability and keeps your spirits up. This sense of progress is incredibly motivating.

I would also like to ask for support, guidance, and encouragement. This could be friends, family, mentors, or colleagues. Sharing your journey with others can provide accountability and a source of motivation. Their support can help you through difficult times and celebrate your successes. Surrounding yourself with a supportive community is essential for maintaining momentum. Remember, you do not have to walk this path alone.

Finally, remember that self-compassion is paramount. Be kind to yourself, especially during setbacks. Do not beat yourself up if you do not make progress as quickly as you had hoped. View setbacks as learning opportunities and continue moving forward. Self-criticism is often counterproductive, a compassionate approach to your shortcomings will enhance your resilience and promote continued motivation. Embrace the process, celebrate the small wins, and remember that progress is not always linear.

Maintaining motivation is a continuous process, not a one-time event. It requires conscious effort, self-awareness, and a willingness to adapt. By incorporating these strategies into your approach, you will be better equipped to navigate the challenges and setbacks that inevitably arise on the path to achieving your goals. Remember, the journey itself is just as important as the destination. Embrace the process, celebrate your achievements, and never give up on your dreams. The power to achieve your goals rests within you, nurturing your motivation unlocks that power. Remember that small, consistent steps, fueled by a commitment to self-reflection, celebration, and adaptability, pave the way toward lasting success and fulfillment. The journey toward your goals is a marathon, not a sprint, and the ability to maintain motivation is what differentiates those who achieve their aspirations from those who do not. Cultivate your inner strength, believe in your capabilities, and remember that perseverance is the key that unlocks the door to your dreams. Your journey is uniquely yours, so celebrate its every step with self-compassion and unwavering determination.

Identifying and Challenging Negative Thoughts

Our journey towards positive thinking continues with a critical step: identifying and challenging the negative thoughts that often hold us back. These negative thought patterns, often subtle and insidious, can significantly impact our emotional state, motivation, and overall well-being. Understanding how these thoughts operate is the first step in dismantling their power and replacing them with more constructive and realistic ones. This process, known as cognitive restructuring, is a powerful tool for enhancing our mental and emotional health.

Negative thoughts rarely arrive in isolation. They frequently manifest in predictable patterns, often fueled by cognitive distortions and systematic errors in thinking that lead to inaccurate and harmful conclusions. These distortions are not intentional lies we tell ourselves, instead, they are ingrained habits of thought that have become deeply rooted over time. Becoming aware of these patterns is crucial to interrupting their cycle and developing more balanced perspectives.

One common cognitive distortion is **all-or-nothing thinking**, also known as black-and-white thinking. This involves seeing things in extremes: success or failure, good or bad, perfect or worthless. For instance, if you do not achieve a perfect score on a test, you might conclude you are a complete failure, overlooking the areas where you performed well. Another related distortion is overgeneralization, where a single adverse event leads to sweeping negative conclusions about oneself or the future. If you experience one rejection, you might believe you will always be rejected.

Mental filtering is another prevalent distortion, where we focus exclusively on negative details while ignoring positive aspects. Imagine receiving positive feedback on a presentation but fixating on one single critical comment, effectively negating the overall positive reception. Similarly, disqualifying the positive involves dismissing positive experiences or feedback as insignificant or irrelevant. You might achieve a significant milestone but dismiss it as "just luck," failing to acknowledge your effort and contribution.

Jumping to conclusions is a broad category encompassing two specific distortions: mind reading and fortune telling. Mind reading involves assuming you know what others are thinking, often negatively. You might believe someone dislikes you based on a single interaction without any concrete evidence. Fortune telling involves predicting adverse outcomes without any factual basis. For example, assuming a project will fail before even starting it is based on a feeling of apprehension.

Magnification and **minimization** involve exaggerating the significance of adverse events while downplaying positive ones. A minor mistake might be blown out of proportion, while significant achievements are minimized or dismissed. This distortion contributes significantly to feelings of inadequacy and self-doubt.

Emotional reasoning involves mistaking feelings for facts. If you feel anxious about a public speaking engagement, you might conclude that you will inevitably fail, disregarding any evidence to the contrary. Finally, should statements involve imposing rigid expectations and rules upon yourself and others, leading to feelings of guilt and self-criticism. These "shoulds" and "musts" often create unnecessary pressure and hinder progress.

Recognizing these cognitive distortions is the first step in challenging them. Once you identify a negative thought, ask yourself: Is this thought accurate? What evidence supports it? What evidence contradicts it? Are there alternative explanations? This process of questioning your negative thoughts promotes a more balanced perspective. You might discover that your negative thoughts are based on assumptions, distortions, or biases rather than on objective reality.

For example, let's revisit the all-or-nothing thinking related to the imperfect test score. Instead of concluding you are a complete failure, you could reframe the situation by acknowledging that, while you did not achieve perfection, you still performed well in certain areas and learned valuable lessons. You could focus on your strengths and the progress you have made rather than fixating on the areas for improvement.

Similarly, if you are experiencing mental filtering, focusing solely on the one negative comment from your presentation, you could actively counteract this by listing all the positive feedback received. Consciously reminding yourself of the overall positive reception can significantly alter your perception of the event, shifting the focus from negativity to accomplishment.

Challenging negative thoughts involves actively replacing them with more realistic and positive ones. This does not necessarily mean suppressing negative feelings entirely but rather replacing the distorted interpretation with a more balanced perspective. This might involve focusing on your strengths, celebrating small victories, and practicing self-compassion.

Another effective technique is reframing, which involves reinterpreting a situation from a different perspective. Instead of focusing on the negative aspects of a challenging task, reframe it as an opportunity for learning and growth. This shift in perspective can change your emotional response and foster a more positive outlook.

Cognitive restructuring is not a quick fix; it requires consistent practice and patience. The more you challenge your negative thoughts, the more adept you become at identifying and replacing them with healthier alternatives. This process enhances your resilience, boosts your self-esteem, and empowers you to approach challenges with a more positive and proactive mindset.

Regular self-reflection, journaling, and mindfulness practices can significantly enhance your ability to recognize and challenge negative thought patterns. Mindfulness, in particular, encourages you to observe your thoughts without judgment, allowing you to become more aware of your mental processes and identify recurring negative patterns. This heightened self-awareness facilitates the process of cognitive restructuring, leading to a more positive and fulfilling life. Remember, positive thinking is not about ignoring negative experiences but about developing a healthier relationship with your thoughts and feelings, empowering you to navigate life's challenges with greater resilience and optimism. The journey towards positive thinking is a continuous process, and each step forward, no matter how small, brings you closer to a more fulfilling and empowered life. Embrace the process, celebrate the progress, and remember that you have the inherent capacity to cultivate a more positive and empowering inner landscape.

Cultivating Gratitude

Cultivating gratitude is not merely a pleasant exercise; it is a powerful tool for reshaping our perspective and fostering a more positive outlook. While challenging negative thoughts is crucial for positive thinking, gratitude acts as an antidote, shifting our focus from what is lacking to what we already possess. It is a conscious effort to appreciate the good in our lives, both big and small, fostering a sense of contentment and well-being that goes beyond the fleeting nature of temporary happiness.

The benefits of practicing gratitude are extensive and well-documented. Research consistently shows a strong correlation between gratitude and increased happiness, improved mental health, and strengthened relationships. When we focus on what we are grateful for, our brains release dopamine and serotonin, neurotransmitters associated with pleasure and well-being. This neurochemical shift contributes to a more positive emotional state, making us more resilient in the face of adversity. Furthermore, gratitude enhances our ability to cope with stress, fostering a sense of perspective and reducing the impact of stressors.

Beyond the individual benefits, gratitude strengthens our social connections. Expressing gratitude to others deepens bonds, fosters empathy, and cultivates a sense of belonging. When we acknowledge and appreciate the contributions of others, we build stronger relationships and enhance the overall social fabric of our lives. This increased social support network acts as a buffer against stress and adversity, contributing significantly to our overall well-being.

Incorporating gratitude into daily life requires intentionality and consistency. It is not simply about passively acknowledging the good; it is about actively cultivating a mindset of appreciation. One of the most effective techniques is keeping a gratitude journal. This simple practice involves regularly writing down things you are grateful for, focusing on the details and the impact they have on your life.

Start with a few minutes each day, reflecting on specific events, people, or possessions that bring you joy or contentment. Describe the experience vividly, focusing on the sensory details, emotions, and impact. For example, instead of simply writing, "I'm grateful for my family," describe a recent event that highlighted the bond you share: a family gathering, a heartfelt conversation, or an act of kindness from a loved one. This level of detail enhances the emotional impact of the practice, deepening your sense of appreciation and fostering a more profound sense of gratitude.

Don't limit yourself to grand gestures or significant events. Gratitude resides in everyday details: a warm cup of coffee on a cold morning, the laughter of a child, the beauty of a sunset, or the support of a friend. These seemingly small moments, when consciously appreciated, can hold immense value and contribute greatly to our well-being. The key is to train your mind to notice these moments and appreciate their positive impact. The more you practice, the more naturally you will begin to notice and value them without the need for conscious effort.

Another powerful technique is expressing appreciation to others. A simple "thank you" can hold immense value, fostering stronger connections and enhancing your overall sense of well-being. Take the time to express your gratitude for the actions and contributions of others, both big and small. Acknowledge their efforts, their support, and their positive impact on your life. This act of appreciation not only strengthens your relationship with them but also reinforces your awareness of the good things in your life. The power of expressing gratitude is undeniable, whether it is directed toward a family member, a friend, a colleague, or a stranger who has positively impacted your day.

Beyond journaling and expressing appreciation, incorporating gratitude into your daily routines can significantly enhance its impact. This might include expressing thanks before meals, reflecting on the positive events of your day each evening, or starting your mornings with a few moments of gratitude. These regular practices, when done consistently, can gradually transform your mindset, increasing your overall positivity and building emotional resilience.

It is crucial to remember that gratitude is not about ignoring or suppressing negative emotions. It is not about pretending that everything is fine or dismissing the real challenges in your life. Instead, gratitude involves intentionally shifting your focus toward what is positive, recognizing both the difficulties and the blessings, and choosing to cultivate appreciation for what you do have. It is about striking a balance between acknowledging reality and fostering a hopeful, appreciative perspective. This kind of outlook helps you meet life's challenges with resilience and optimism.

Furthermore, cultivating gratitude is a continuous process, not a destination. There will be days when gratitude comes easily and others when it feels like a struggle. Life will present difficulties, making it harder to maintain a positive perspective. During those times, remember that gratitude is not about being perfect but about showing up consistently with kindness toward yourself. If you fall out of practice, do not be discouraged. Simply return to it, remind yourself of its value, and resume with a spirit of compassion. Consistency, not perfection, brings lasting transformation.

It is also important to be realistic and authentic in your practice. Do not force yourself to feel grateful for things you do not genuinely appreciate. Focus instead on aspects of your life that truly bring you joy or comfort, even if they are small. Authenticity matters. Forced gratitude loses its emotional impact, whereas genuine appreciation, no matter how simple, nourishes your well-being. Look for those real moments of thankfulness and let them ground your practice.

In addition to journaling and expressing appreciation, many other activities can promote gratitude. Spending time in nature, engaging in activities that bring you joy, connecting with loved ones, and practicing mindfulness can all enhance your ability to appreciate the positive aspects of your life. These activities provide opportunities to engage with the world actively and consciously recognize the good experiences that come your way. Mindfulness, in particular, strengthens your awareness of the present moment, allowing you to fully appreciate the sensory details and emotions that accompany those moments.

In conclusion, cultivating gratitude is a powerful tool for transforming your perspective and enhancing your overall well-being. It is a proactive practice that requires intentionality and consistency, but the rewards are profound. By incorporating gratitude into your daily life, you not only elevate your emotional state and resilience but also deepen your relationships and develop a greater appreciation for life's experiences, both large and small. The journey of cultivating gratitude is ongoing, one that calls for continuous commitment and self-compassion, yet it is deeply rewarding. Remember, true strength does not lie in avoiding hardship but in facing it with a grateful heart and a resilient mindset. The regular practice of gratitude enables you to value the journey, learn from its trials, and celebrate its victories, nurturing a sense of fulfillment and joy that goes beyond temporary happiness. Embrace the power of gratitude. It is a gift you give to yourself and a gift that radiates outward to those around you.

Practicing Optimism

Practicing optimism isn't about ignoring reality or pretending everything is perfect. It's about cultivating a mindset that allows you to see possibilities, even in the face of adversity. It's a conscious choice to focus on potential solutions rather than dwelling on problems, and to anticipate positive outcomes rather than expecting the worst. This proactive approach to life significantly impacts our resilience, our ability to bounce back from setbacks, and our overall well-being.

The foundation of optimism lies in a belief in your ability to influence your future. This isn't about naivete, it's about acknowledging your agency and your capacity to make choices and take actions that shape your destiny. It's about understanding that while you may not be able to control everything that happens to you, you can control how you respond, how you interpret events, and the actions you take in response. This sense of agency is pivotal in fostering resilience. When confronted with challenges, an optimist focuses on what they can control rather than dwelling on what they can't.

Optimism, however, is not about unrealistic positive thinking. It's not about burying your head in the sand and ignoring potential problems. Realistic optimism involves acknowledging challenges while maintaining a belief in your capacity to overcome them. It's about a balanced perspective that embraces both the realities of life and the potential for positive change. Unrealistic optimism, on the other hand, can be detrimental. It can lead to unpreparedness, a lack of contingency planning, and ultimately, increased vulnerability when things inevitably go wrong. Realistic optimism, therefore, is about finding a healthy middle ground, a perspective that is grounded in reality but infused with a positive expectation for the future.

One powerful technique for cultivating optimism is reframing negative thoughts. This involves consciously challenging negative self-talk and replacing it with more positive and constructive interpretations. When faced with a setback, instead of focusing on the negative aspects, consciously shift your perspective to highlight potential learning opportunities, alternative solutions, or positive aspects of the experience. For example, if a project fails, instead of focusing on the failure itself, focus on what you learned from the experience, what you would do differently next time, and the potential for growth and improvement. This reframing process is essential for building resilience and maintaining a positive outlook.

Another crucial element of practicing optimism is setting realistic goals and expectations. Setting unattainable goals can lead to frustration and disappointment, undermining optimism. Instead, focus on setting smaller, achievable goals that build momentum and contribute to a sense of accomplishment. Breaking down larger tasks into smaller, manageable steps makes the overall objective seem less daunting and increases the likelihood of success. This incremental approach fosters a sense of progress, reinforcing the belief in your ability to achieve your goals. Celebrate each small victory along the way, acknowledge your progress, and appreciate your efforts. This positive reinforcement strengthens your optimistic outlook.

Visualization is another effective tool for cultivating optimism. This involves mentally rehearsing successful outcomes. By vividly imagining yourself achieving your goals, you prime your mind for success and enhance your belief in your ability to achieve them. This mental rehearsal strengthens your confidence, reducing anxiety and increasing your resilience in the face of challenges. Regular visualization, combined with positive affirmations, can significantly enhance your optimistic outlook. The key is to engage all your senses, sight, sound, smell, touch, and taste, to create a truly immersive experience.

Furthermore, fostering self-compassion is essential for cultivating optimism. Treat yourself with the same kindness and understanding you would offer a friend facing similar challenges. Avoid self-criticism and negative self-talk. Instead, focus on self-encouragement and self-acceptance. When you make a mistake, view it as an opportunity for learning and growth rather than a personal failure. This self-compassionate approach strengthens your resilience and fosters a more positive outlook.

Surrounding yourself with positive influences is equally essential. Spend time with people who uplift and encourage you, and who offer support and understanding. Limit your exposure to negativity and toxic relationships. The people you spend time with significantly influence your outlook on life, and surrounding yourself with optimistic individuals can significantly enhance your optimism. This positive social support network acts as a buffer against stress and adversity, reinforcing your optimistic belief in your ability to overcome challenges.

Beyond social support, practicing mindfulness can enhance your optimism. Mindfulness involves focusing on the present moment without judgment. By consciously directing your attention to the present, you reduce your tendency to dwell on past failures or worry about future uncertainties. This present-moment awareness allows you to appreciate the positive aspects of your current experience, enhancing your sense of gratitude and contentment. This fosters a more balanced perspective, reducing anxiety and increasing your capacity for optimism.

Regular exercise also plays a significant role in cultivating optimism. Physical activity releases endorphins, which have mood-boosting effects. Exercise not only improves physical health but also enhances mental well-being, reducing stress and anxiety, and fostering a more positive outlook. The sense of accomplishment derived from regular physical activity further reinforces optimism and strengthens resilience. Find an activity you enjoy, whether it's running, swimming, yoga, or dancing, and make it a regular part of your routine.

Finally, maintaining a healthy lifestyle, including adequate sleep, a balanced diet, and mindful stress management, is essential for sustaining optimism. When your physical and mental health is compromised, your capacity for optimism diminishes. Prioritizing self-care ensures you have the energy and resilience to face life's challenges with a positive outlook. This self-care is not a luxury, it's an investment in your overall well-being, including your capacity for optimism.

Cultivating optimism is a continuous journey, not a destination. There will be times when maintaining a positive outlook feels challenging. Life inevitably presents setbacks, and it's during these times that the practice of optimism is most crucial. Remember that setbacks are temporary, and your capacity for resilience is far greater than you may realize. By consistently practicing the techniques outlined above, you'll gradually strengthen your optimistic outlook and enhance your ability to navigate life's inevitable challenges with resilience and hope. Embrace the journey, celebrate small victories, and never underestimate the power of a positive mindset. The path to optimism is a journey of continuous growth, self-discovery, and resilience. It's a path that leads to a more prosperous, more fulfilling life.

Visualizing Success

Visualizing success isn't merely daydreaming, it's a powerful mental rehearsal that primes your mind for achievement. It's about actively engaging your imagination to create vivid mental pictures of yourself accomplishing your goals, experiencing the positive emotions associated with success, and feeling the tangible rewards. This process taps into the brain's neuroplasticity, strengthening the neural pathways associated with positive outcomes and bolstering your belief in your capabilities.

Think of visualization as a mental dry run. Just as athletes mentally rehearse their performance before a competition, visualizing success allows you to practice the actions, emotions, and outcomes associated with your goals in a safe, controlled environment. This mental preparation reduces anxiety, builds confidence, and improves performance. It allows you to anticipate potential challenges and develop strategies for overcoming them before you even encounter them in the real world.

Effective visualization requires a conscious and deliberate effort. It's not about passively letting images drift through your mind, it's about actively creating a detailed, multi-sensory experience. Engage all five senses:

Sight: See yourself achieving your goal. Imagine the vibrant colors, the intricate details, and the overall scene. If your goal is to give a successful presentation, you should see the audience engaged and attentive, the slide show working flawlessly, and your confident demeanor. If your goal is to run a marathon, visualize the course, the cheering crowds, and the feeling of crossing the finish line.

Sound: Hear the sounds associated with success. If your goal involves a public speaking engagement, hear the appreciative applause. If you're aiming for a promotion, hear the congratulatory words of your boss. If you're striving for a healthier lifestyle, hear the rhythmic sound of your breath during exercise.

Touch: Feel the physical sensations associated with accomplishment. Feel the weight of that award in your hand, the comfortable texture of your new clothing after achieving a weight loss goal, and the firmness of the ground beneath your feet as you conquer a challenging hike.

Smell: Imagine the scents that accompany your success. The fresh morning air after a run, the delicious aroma of a celebratory dinner, or the smell of new books if your goal is to write a novel.

Taste: Savor the taste of victory. The celebratory champagne, the delightful meal you enjoy after achieving a significant milestone, or the satisfying taste of your homemade meal if your goal is to improve your cooking skills.

The more vivid and detailed your visualization, the more powerful its effect. The key is to immerse yourself entirely in the experience, making it as realistic as possible. Regular practice enhances the effectiveness of visualization. Aim for daily sessions, even if they are only for a few minutes. Consistency is key to seeing tangible results.

Beyond visualizing the end goal, it's equally important to visualize the steps necessary to achieve it. Break down significant, daunting goals into smaller, manageable steps. Visualize yourself completing each step, building momentum and confidence as you progress. This incremental approach minimizes feelings of overwhelm and fosters a sense of accomplishment along the way, strengthening your belief in your ability to achieve the larger goal.

Another crucial aspect of effective visualization is focusing on positive emotions. Visualize not only the outcome but also the positive feelings associated with it: joy, pride, satisfaction, and gratitude. Feel the surge of accomplishment, the sense of empowerment, and the deep satisfaction of realizing your dreams. By associating your goals with positive emotions, you create a powerful internal reward system that motivates you to persevere and overcome challenges.

However, visualization is not a substitute for action. It's a powerful tool to complement your efforts, not to replace them. Visualization enhances your motivation, focus, and confidence, making it easier to take the necessary steps to achieve your goals. It works best when combined with a clear action plan and consistent effort. It's about creating a synergistic relationship between your mental preparation and your physical actions.

It's also important to acknowledge and address any opposing thoughts or doubts that may arise during the visualization process. Don't suppress these feelings, instead, acknowledge them, challenge their validity, and replace them with positive affirmations and encouraging self-talk. This process strengthens your resilience and reinforces your belief in your ability to overcome challenges.

Visualization can also be used to improve self-confidence in specific situations. If you struggle with public speaking, for instance, visualize yourself delivering a confident and engaging presentation. Imagine yourself handling questions effectively, connecting with the audience, and feeling a sense of accomplishment after a successful speech. This mental rehearsal helps to desensitize you to the anxiety-inducing aspects of public speaking, improving your performance and building your confidence.

The power of visualization extends beyond specific goals; it can also be used to foster a general sense of self-efficacy and optimism. Visualize yourself handling stress effectively, overcoming obstacles with grace, and responding to challenges with resilience. This ongoing practice builds your overall confidence, strengthening your ability to face life's inevitable ups and downs with positivity and determination. It creates a mental framework for handling adversity, reinforcing your belief in your ability to navigate life's challenges and emerge more substantial and more resilient.

Also, consider using visualization techniques in conjunction with other positive thinking strategies like affirmations and gratitude practices. Affirmations strengthen your belief in your abilities, while gratitude enhances your appreciation for your current circumstances and nurtures a more optimistic outlook. When combined with visualization, these techniques create a potent synergy, enhancing your overall well-being and accelerating your progress toward your goals.

In conclusion, visualization is a powerful tool for achieving success and enhancing self-confidence. By actively engaging your imagination, creating vivid mental images, and focusing on positive emotions, you can prime your mind for achievement and strengthen your belief in your abilities. Remember, visualization is most effective when combined with a clear action plan, consistent effort, and a positive, optimistic outlook. Make it a regular part of your routine and experience the transformative power of visualizing your success. Embrace the journey and watch your dreams unfold. The path to success is paved with consistent effort, positive thinking, and an unwavering belief in your potential, all of which are amplified by the power of visualization.

Affirmations and Positive Self-Talk

Affirmations and positive self-talk are potent tools for cultivating a positive mindset and building unshakeable self-belief. They act as internal motivators, subtly reshaping our subconscious perceptions and replacing negative thought patterns with empowering, constructive ones. Think of them as mental vitamins, nourishing your self-esteem and confidence on a daily basis. Unlike visualization, which focuses on external goals, affirmations work directly on your internal narrative, the constant stream of thoughts and self-assessments that shape your self-image.

The power of affirmations lies in their ability to reprogram your subconscious mind. Repeatedly affirming positive statements, even if initially felt untrue, gradually rewire your neural pathways, making those positive beliefs more ingrained and accessible. It's a process of neuroplasticity, where your brain literally reshapes itself in response to repeated mental stimulation. This isn't about fooling yourself, it's about gently guiding your mind toward a more empowering perspective, fostering a belief in your inherent capabilities and worth.

Creating effective affirmations requires careful consideration. They should be:

Positive: Focus on what you want, not what you don't want. Instead of "I won't be late," try "I will arrive on time." Instead of "I'm not afraid," use "I feel confident and capable." Negative phrasing can actually reinforce the very thing you're trying to avoid.

Present Tense: Phrase affirmations as if they are already confirmed. Use the present tense to instill a sense of immediate empowerment. "I am confident" is more effective than "I will be confident." The present tense anchors the affirmation in your current reality, making it feel more tangible and believable.

Specific and Measurable: Vague affirmations are less effective. Instead of "I am successful," try saying, "I am achieving my goals with consistent effort and determination." Specificity increases the impact and allows for more focused mental rehearsal.

Personal: Your affirmations should resonate with you. Don't adopt generic statements; you can craft affirmations that are specifically tailored to your needs, goals, and aspirations. What areas of your life need the most positive reinforcement? What beliefs do you want to solidify?

Emotionally Charged: Infuse your affirmations with feeling. When you repeat your affirmations, feel the emotion associated with them. If you're affirming your courage, feel a surge of bravery. If you're affirming your self-worth, feel a sense of deep self-acceptance. The emotional connection amplifies the power of your affirmations.

Here are some examples of effective affirmations across various life domains:

For Self-Esteem and Self-Acceptance:

"I am worthy of love and happiness."

"I embrace my imperfections and celebrate my strengths."

"I am confident in my abilities and talents."

"I am kind and compassionate towards myself."

"I forgive myself for past mistakes and learn from them."

"I am capable of achieving great things."

"I am enough, just as I am."

"I love and accept myself unconditionally."

"My self-worth is not dependent on external validation."

"I am strong, resilient, and capable of overcoming any challenge."

For Confidence and Achievement:

"I am confident and capable in all that I do."

"I approach challenges with enthusiasm and determination."

"I am resourceful and find creative solutions to problems."

"I am focused and determined to achieve my goals."

"I am a successful and productive individual."

"I am persistent and never give up on my dreams."

"I attract opportunities that align with my goals."

"I am worthy of success and abundance."

"I am confident in my public speaking abilities."

"I am a skilled communicator and connect easily with others."

For Health and Well-being:

"I am healthy, strong, and full of vitality."

"My body is strong and resilient."

"I nourish my body with healthy foods and regular exercise."

"I make choices that support my physical and mental well-being."

"I am grateful for my health and well-being."

"I am committed to living a healthy and balanced lifestyle."

"I am peaceful and calm, even in stressful situations."

"I manage stress effectively and maintain emotional balance."

"I prioritize self-care and make time for relaxation."

"I am filled with energy and enthusiasm for life."

Integrating Affirmations into Your Daily Routine:

The effectiveness of affirmations is directly linked to consistency. Make it a habit to repeat your chosen affirmations several times a day, ideally at times when your mind is receptive and calm. Consider incorporating them into your morning routine, before bed, during meditation, or any other time you have a few minutes of quiet contemplation.

You can write your affirmations down and post them where you'll see them regularly, on your mirror, your refrigerator, or your computer screen. Reading them aloud adds an extra layer of impact, engaging both your visual and auditory senses. You can even record yourself saying your affirmations and listen to them throughout the day.

It's essential to feel the affirmations, not just say them mechanically. Close your eyes, take a deep breath, and visualize the feelings and experiences associated with your affirmations. Let the words sink in and resonate with your inner being. Believe in their truth, even if it initially feels like a stretch. The more sincere your repetition, the more effective the process will be.

Positive self-talk operates on a similar principle but is more spontaneous and responsive to immediate situations. It's about consciously replacing negative thoughts with positive, encouraging ones. Whenever you catch yourself thinking negatively, challenge that thought and replace it with a more empowering alternative.

For instance, if you make a mistake, instead of berating yourself ("I'm so stupid!"), say something supportive like, "This is a learning opportunity, and I'll do better next time." Instead of focusing on failures, highlight your strengths and past successes.

Positive self-talk is like having an internal cheerleader, consistently reminding you of your capabilities and encouraging you to persevere. It's a skill that takes practice, but with consistent effort, you'll become more adept at identifying and replacing negative self-talk with constructive and encouraging alternatives. It's about building a habit of self-compassion and self-encouragement.

Remember, affirmations and positive self-talk are not magic wands that instantly erase negative beliefs. They are tools that, when used consistently and with intention, can gradually reshape your thinking patterns, leading to a more positive, confident, and empowered self. Combine them with visualization, gratitude practices, and other positive thinking techniques to create a comprehensive approach to cultivating a resilient and optimistic mindset. The journey towards self-improvement is a marathon, not a sprint, and these tools will provide invaluable support along the way. Embrace the process, be patient with yourself, and celebrate your progress every step of the way. Your potential is limitless, and with consistent effort and a positive mindset, you can achieve anything you set your mind to.

The Importance of Self Forgiveness

The journey towards a more fulfilling and empowered life often involves confronting our past mistakes and learning to forgive ourselves. Self-forgiveness is not about condoning harmful actions, instead, it's about releasing the burden of self-criticism and self-blame that prevents us from moving forward. Holding onto guilt and regret can be incredibly debilitating, creating a cycle of negativity that undermines our self-esteem and hinders our personal growth. It's a crucial step in the process of emotional healing and self-acceptance, paving the way for a more peaceful and joyful future.

Many of us struggle with self-forgiveness because we tend to judge ourselves far more harshly than we would judge others in similar situations. We hold onto past mistakes, replaying them in our minds, fueling feelings of shame and inadequacy. This internal critic, ever-present and judgmental, prevents us from acknowledging our growth and progress. We forget that we are all works in progress, constantly evolving and learning from our experiences. Every mistake is an opportunity for growth, a chance to learn and become a better version of ourselves. Yet, we often fail to see this, trapped in the cycle of self-recrimination.

The first step towards self-forgiveness is acknowledging the role of our past experiences in shaping our present selves. Understanding the context of our mistakes, recognizing the factors that contributed to them, and acknowledging the impact of those experiences are paramount. Often, mistakes are not simply isolated incidents, but rather the result of complex circumstances, including our upbringing, past traumas, and the pressures of life. Acknowledging these contributing factors allows us to approach our past with compassion and understanding rather than harsh judgment. This process is not about excusing harmful behavior, but about understanding its origins and accepting that our past actions do not define who we are today.

Another critical aspect of self-forgiveness is accepting responsibility for our actions. This doesn't mean dwelling on guilt or self-blame, instead, it involves acknowledging our role in the events and taking ownership of our choices. Acceptance, in this context, is about acknowledging the truth of our past without being defined by it. It's a process of owning our mistakes without letting them dictate our future. This act of taking responsibility is empowering, it demonstrates self-awareness and a commitment to personal growth. It frees us from the need to justify our actions or make excuses for our past selves.

Once we've acknowledged our mistakes and accepted responsibility, we can begin the process of letting go. This is often the most challenging aspect of self-forgiveness, as it requires us to release the emotional burden of guilt and regret. Holding onto these negative emotions only serves to perpetuate suffering. It's like carrying a heavy weight on our shoulders, preventing us from moving forward. Letting go involves actively choosing to release the negativity associated with our past mistakes, freeing ourselves from the shackles of self-blame. It's a conscious decision to move forward and embrace a more positive future.

Several techniques can assist in letting go of self-criticism and embracing self-acceptance. Journaling can provide a valuable outlet for processing emotions and gaining perspective. Writing about our mistakes and the feelings they evoke can be a cathartic experience, helping us to understand our thoughts and feelings more clearly.

Through journaling, we can begin to reframe our narratives, replacing self-critical thoughts with more compassionate and understanding ones.

Meditation and mindfulness practices can also be highly beneficial. By focusing on the present moment, we can detach from the grip of the past and cultivate a sense of inner peace. Mindfulness exercises help us to observe our thoughts and emotions without judgment, allowing us to create space between ourselves and our negative self-talk. This distance provides an opportunity to approach our mistakes with greater compassion and understanding.

Practicing self-compassion is another crucial step. Self-compassion involves treating ourselves with the same kindness and understanding that we would offer a friend in a similar situation. Instead of berating ourselves for our past mistakes, we acknowledge our imperfections, recognizing that we are all flawed human beings, and that making mistakes is part of the human experience. This approach softens the harshness of self-criticism and creates a space for self-acceptance and growth.

Forgiveness is not a one-time event, it's a process that unfolds over time. It requires consistent effort and a willingness to engage in self-reflection and emotional processing. There may be setbacks along the way, moments when old patterns of self-criticism resurface. It is essential to be patient and compassionate with ourselves during these times, recognizing that the journey towards self-forgiveness is not always linear. It's a winding path with ups and downs, but with consistent practice, we can gradually cultivate a greater sense of self-acceptance and emotional freedom.

Self-forgiveness is not just about releasing the past, it is about creating a brighter future. When we forgive ourselves, we free ourselves from the weight of past mistakes, allowing us to focus our energy on creating a life that aligns with our values and aspirations. This creates a positive feedback loop, boosting self-esteem, fostering resilience, and empowering us to move forward with confidence and optimism. The act of self-forgiveness is an act of self-love and self-respect, laying the foundation for a healthier and more fulfilling life.

It's vital to remember that self-forgiveness isn't about forgetting or ignoring our past mistakes. It's about acknowledging them, learning from them, and choosing to move forward without the burden of self-blame. It's a process of integrating those experiences into our lives, allowing them to contribute to our personal growth and development without controlling our present or future.

To further enhance the journey of self-forgiveness, consider incorporating these practical exercises into your daily routine:

The "Kindness Letter" Exercise: Write a letter to your past self, expressing understanding and compassion for the mistakes you made. Please let me know the challenges you faced and the lessons you learned. This exercise helps to shift your perspective from self-criticism to self-compassion.

The "Gratitude Reflection": Focus on the positive aspects of your life and the things you are grateful for. Gratitude helps to shift your focus away from negativity and also fosters a sense of appreciation for your present circumstances.

Mindful Breathing and Body Scan: Practice mindful breathing exercises and body scans to connect with the present moment and release tension held in the body. Physical tension is often associated with emotional stress, and relaxation techniques can help to alleviate both.

Remember, self-forgiveness is a personal journey, and the pace at which you progress will be unique to you. There's no right or wrong way to forgive yourself, the key is to approach the process with kindness, compassion, and a commitment to self-growth. Embrace the journey, be patient with yourself, and celebrate your progress along the way. The ability to forgive ourselves is a powerful testament to our resilience, our capacity for growth, and our inherent worth. It's a crucial step towards building a life filled with peace, joy, and lasting fulfillment. The path to self-forgiveness is a path towards a more compassionate, accepting, and ultimately, more joyful you. It's a journey well worth undertaking.

Forgiving Others

Forgiving others is a profound act of self-care, often perceived as a gift bestowed solely upon the recipient. However, the truth is far more nuanced. Forgiveness, in its most accurate form, is a journey of liberation for the forgiver, a release from the chains of resentment and anger that bind us to the past. Holding onto bitterness and anger consumes our energy, poisoning our present and hindering our future. It's a heavy burden, far heavier than any perceived transgression warrants. This section explores the intricate process of extending forgiveness, understanding its complexities, and harnessing its transformative power.

The initial hurdle in forgiving others is often the belief that forgiveness equates to condoning harmful actions. This misconception prevents many from even considering the possibility of letting go. Forgiveness isn't about excusing the behavior, it's about releasing the grip that the past has on your present emotional well-being. It's about recognizing that holding onto anger and resentment serves only to perpetuate your suffering. The person who wronged you may not even be aware of the emotional turmoil they've caused, or perhaps they are completely indifferent. Regardless, their actions and their potential lack of remorse shouldn't dictate the trajectory of your emotional health.

Consider the physical manifestation of anger and resentment. Do you clench your jaw, feel the tension in your shoulders, or experience stomach discomfort? These physical symptoms are direct consequences of prolonged negative emotions. Forgiveness acts as an antidote, a release of this toxic emotional burden. It's a conscious choice to unburden yourself, to reclaim your emotional sovereignty. This isn't a passive acceptance, it's an active decision to prioritize your own mental and emotional health.

The process of forgiving others isn't always a swift, clean break. It's a journey, often winding and uneven, filled with moments of progress and occasional setbacks. There will be days when the hurt resurfaces, and when the memories re-emerge with vivid intensity. This is perfectly normal. It is part of the healing process. Acknowledge these feelings without judgment. Recognize them for what they are, remnants of the past attempting to regain control. Please do not allow them to define you or derail your progress.

One effective strategy for navigating these moments of resurgence is mindfulness. When feelings of anger or resentment arise, pause. Take a deep breath. Observe the emotions without judgment, acknowledging their presence without succumbing to them. Visualize these feelings as clouds passing across the sky, they are transient, temporary phenomena that will eventually drift away. This mindful approach helps to create emotional distance, preventing you from being completely overwhelmed by the intensity of the emotion.

Journaling can also be a potent tool. Writing about your experiences and expressing your anger and hurt can be a cathartic process. Allow yourself to explore your emotions on paper fully. I suggest that you. Don't censor yourself. Pour your heart out. Through this process of articulation, you begin to externalize your emotions, making them less overwhelming and easier to manage. Once you've expressed your feelings, you can begin to reflect on them, gaining perspective and understanding.

Another helpful technique is to reframe your narrative. Instead of focusing solely on the harm caused, I would suggest that you consider the broader context. Were there mitigating factors? What was the other person's perspective? This doesn't excuse harmful behavior, but it can broaden your understanding and foster empathy. Empathy, even for those who have wronged you, can be a significant step towards forgiveness. Remember, you are not obligated to forget, only to release the grip of resentment.

Forgiveness often requires understanding the root of your anger and resentment. What specific needs were unmet? What values were violated? Identifying these unmet needs and violated values can provide clarity and empower you to take steps to meet those needs and uphold those values in your own life. This process is not about seeking revenge or reconciliation with the other person, it's about reclaiming your power and well-being.

Consider the concept of compassion. While it may seem challenging to extend compassion to someone who has hurt you, understanding their struggles and challenges can often soften the heart. Everyone carries their burdens, everyone makes mistakes. By acknowledging their humanity, even with their flaws, you can begin to move toward forgiveness. This is not about excusing their behavior, but about releasing the need to hold onto the anger and resentment that it fuels within you.

Forgiveness is not a sign of weakness, it's an act of immense strength. It takes courage to confront your pain, to acknowledge your hurt, and to consciously choose to release the burden of resentment. It's a testament to your emotional resilience and your capacity for growth. Remember that it is a process, not a destination, and that setbacks are inevitable. Be patient with yourself and compassionate with your journey.

In cases where reconciliation is possible and desired, it's crucial to approach it with clear boundaries. Forgiveness does not imply condoning past actions or inviting further harm. It means choosing to move forward while maintaining your safety and well-being. Open communication, setting boundaries, and focusing on the present are key components of any potential reconciliation. Please remember that reconciliation is not a prerequisite for forgiveness.

Ultimately, forgiveness is about reclaiming your peace of mind. It's about freeing yourself from the prison of resentment and anger and stepping into a future unburdened by the past. It's an investment in your emotional well-being, a profound act of self-love, and a crucial step on the path to a more fulfilling and empowered life. It's about creating space for joy, peace, and healing, not just for yourself but for your overall well-being. It's a powerful act of self-compassion. The journey of forgiveness is a journey towards a more peaceful and joyful you. Embrace the journey, be kind to yourself, and celebrate each small step you take towards liberation.

Letting Go of the Past

Letting go of the past isn't about forgetting, it's about freeing yourself from its grip. It's about acknowledging the pain, learning from the experiences, and consciously choosing to move forward. This process requires active participation and a willingness to engage in self-compassionate practices. Holding onto past hurts, resentments, and regrets is like carrying a heavy backpack filled with stones. It weighs you down, slows your progress, and prevents you from enjoying the journey. Unburdening yourself is the first crucial step toward creating a brighter, more fulfilling future.

One of the most effective strategies for letting go is mindfulness. Mindfulness is the practice of paying attention to the present moment without judgment. When painful memories or emotions surface, instead of getting swept away by them, take a moment to acknowledge their presence. Observe them as you would observe clouds drifting across the sky, which are transient phenomena that will eventually pass. Don't try to suppress or ignore these feelings, allow them to be without engaging with them emotionally. This creates a sense of distance and helps prevent you from being overwhelmed.

A practical mindfulness exercise involves focusing on your breath. When a wave of sadness, anger, or regret washes over you, gently bring your attention to your breath. Feel the air entering and leaving your body. Notice the sensation of the breath against your nostrils, the rise and fall of your chest or abdomen. This simple act can anchor you in the present moment, grounding you and reducing the intensity of the past's hold. You can enhance this practice by incorporating a body scan meditation, systematically bringing awareness to different parts of your body, noticing any tension or discomfort, and consciously releasing it. This helps to connect you to your physical self, which can offer a sense of stability and security amidst turbulent emotions.

Incorporating mindfulness into your daily routine, even for just a few minutes, can significantly impact your ability to manage challenging emotions and let go of the past. Start by practicing mindfulness during simple tasks, such as eating or washing dishes. Pay attention to the sensations, the tastes, the textures. This helps train your mind to focus on the present, gradually reducing its tendency to dwell on the past. The more you practice, the stronger your ability to remain present and manage the emotional impact of past experiences. Regular mindfulness meditation, even 10 to 15 minutes daily, can be transformative in cultivating this capacity.

Another powerful tool for letting go is journaling. Writing about your experiences, both the positive and the negative, allows you to process your emotions in a safe and controlled environment. You don't need to worry about grammar or structure, just let your thoughts and feelings flow onto the page. This act of expressing yourself can be incredibly cathartic, helping to release pent-up emotions and gain a new perspective on your past. Journaling also offers a tangible record of your journey, allowing you to track your progress and celebrate your achievements along the way. Reviewing past journal entries can highlight the significant personal growth and resilience you have demonstrated.

When journaling, consider exploring the narratives you tell yourself about past events. Often, we unconsciously reinforce negative patterns of thinking, perpetuating feelings of guilt, shame, or resentment. Journaling provides an opportunity to challenge these narratives, examining them with a more compassionate and objective lens. For example, if you're struggling to forgive yourself for a past mistake, ask yourself: what have I learned from this experience? What steps can I take to prevent this from happening again?

Reframing your narrative can transform feelings of self-blame into valuable lessons and opportunities for growth.

In addition to journaling, engaging in creative expression can be a powerful way to release the emotional weight of the past. Whether it's painting, sculpting, playing music, or writing poetry, creative activities offer an outlet for emotions that may be difficult to articulate through words alone. The act of creation allows you to transform pain and frustration into something beautiful and meaningful. This process can be profoundly therapeutic, fostering a sense of self-discovery and personal empowerment. It's not about creating a masterpiece, it's about expressing yourself authentically, allowing your emotions to find their voice.

Physical activity also plays a vital role in letting go of the past. Exercise releases endorphins, which have mood-boosting effects. Regular physical activity, whether it's a brisk walk, a yoga session, or a more strenuous workout, can help reduce stress, improve sleep, and enhance overall well-being. Physical exertion can be a metaphor for releasing the burdens you've been carrying, allowing you to move more freely and confidently into the future. The focus required during physical activity also provides a break from rumination on past events, offering a mental respite.

Setting realistic goals can further aid in this process. When overwhelmed by the weight of the past, it's easy to become paralyzed by inaction. Setting small, achievable goals, however seemingly insignificant, helps to restore a sense of control and accomplishment. The accomplishment of these small victories builds momentum and provides a sense of progress, fostering a more positive outlook on the future. Focus on what you can control, celebrating every step forward, no matter how small.

Remember that letting go is a process, not a destination. There will be moments when the past resurfaces, when painful memories or emotions re-emerge. This is perfectly normal, it's part of the healing journey. Acknowledge these feelings without judgment, allowing yourself to experience them entirely, but don't let them define you. Use the tools you've developed, mindfulness, journaling, creative expression, and physical activity to navigate these challenging moments. Be patient with yourself, and celebrate your progress along the way. The key is not to erase the past, but to learn from it and move forward with greater understanding and compassion.

Forgiveness, both of others and of yourself, is a crucial element in releasing the past. It's not about condoning harmful actions, but about freeing yourself from the burden of resentment and anger. Forgiveness allows you to reclaim your emotional energy and focus on creating a positive future. Self-forgiveness requires acknowledging your mistakes, learning from them, and choosing to move forward. This is a powerful act of self-compassion, allowing you to break free from the cycle of self-criticism and self-blame.

Cultivating self-compassion is essential throughout this process. Treat yourself with the same kindness and understanding you would offer a close friend. Acknowledge your struggles and imperfections without judgment, recognizing that everyone makes mistakes and experiences setbacks. Self-compassion allows you to navigate the challenges of letting go with greater resilience and strength. It enables you to move forward, not with guilt or shame, but with hope and optimism.

Finally, remember that you are not alone. Seeking support from friends, family, or a therapist can be invaluable during this process. Sharing your experiences with others can provide perspective, validation, and a sense of connection. A therapist can provide guidance and support, helping you develop coping mechanisms and navigate challenging emotions. Don't hesitate to reach out for help when needed, it's a sign of strength, not weakness. Letting go of the past is a journey, not a race. Take your time, be patient with yourself, and celebrate each small step you take toward a brighter future. The path to healing and liberation is worth the effort.

Breaking Free from Toxic Relationships

Breaking free from a toxic relationship is a courageous act, a testament to your self-respect and commitment to your well-being. It's a journey that often requires immense strength, resilience, and a willingness to confront brutal truths. Many find themselves trapped in these cycles, bound by a complex web of emotions, dependencies, and ingrained patterns of behavior. Understanding the dynamics of toxic relationships is the first crucial step toward achieving freedom.

A consistent pattern of negativity, emotional manipulation, and disrespect characterizes toxic relationships. These relationships aren't always overtly abusive, they can be subtle and insidious, eroding your self-esteem and sense of self-worth over time. One common trait is control, the attempt to dictate your choices, your actions, and even your thoughts. This control can manifest in various ways, from subtle gaslighting, where your perceptions and reality are questioned and undermined, to overt threats and intimidation.

Another hallmark is emotional manipulation, where your feelings are used against you. This might involve guilt-tripping, making you feel responsible for the other person's emotions, or playing the victim to garner sympathy and control. Constant criticism, belittling, and insults also erode your self-confidence and sense of self-worth. These behaviors chip away at your self-esteem, leaving you feeling inadequate, confused, and unsure of yourself. The constant negativity creates an environment of stress and anxiety, draining your energy and impacting your overall well-being.

Lack of respect is another key indicator. A toxic relationship often lacks basic courtesy, consideration, and empathy. Your needs, feelings, and opinions are consistently disregarded or dismissed. You might find yourself constantly walking on eggshells, fearing the other person's unpredictable reactions or outbursts. Healthy relationships are built on mutual respect, understanding, and compromise. In contrast, toxic relationships are characterized by an imbalance of power, leaving one partner feeling dominated and controlled.

Recognizing these signs is a significant step toward liberation. However, leaving a toxic relationship is rarely a simple decision. Years of emotional conditioning can create a sense of dependence and fear of the unknown. The fear of being alone, the hope for things to improve, and the belief that you are somehow responsible for the toxicity are all common reasons why people stay longer than they should. But remember, your happiness is not contingent on remaining within it.

Breaking free requires a plan. The first step involves setting clear boundaries. Boundaries are essential for protecting your emotional and mental health. These boundaries might involve limiting contact, refusing to participate in emotionally damaging conversations, or simply saying "no" to requests that compromise your well-being. Setting boundaries is an act of self-respect, asserting your right to be treated with dignity and consideration.

It's crucial to remember that setting boundaries isn't selfish, it's self-preservation. You are not obligated to tolerate abusive behavior or to sacrifice your well-being for the sake of another. Enforce these boundaries consistently, even when faced with resistance or criticism. Your boundaries are not up for negotiation, they represent your commitment to safeguarding your mental and emotional health. It's essential to clearly communicate your boundaries, explaining the reasons behind them calmly and firmly. Preparation is key, rehearse what you'll say to minimize emotional reactivity during challenging conversations.

A critical aspect of leaving a toxic relationship is building a support system. This support network could involve friends, family members, or professional therapists. Confiding in trusted individuals can provide crucial emotional support, validation, and a sense of perspective. They can offer a listening ear, unbiased advice, and a reminder of your strength and worth. Talking about your experiences can be incredibly cathartic, helping you process your emotions and gain clarity.

Professional support from a therapist or counselor is often invaluable. A therapist can provide a safe and confidential space to explore the complexities of the relationship, understand your feelings, and develop healthy coping mechanisms. They can help you identify underlying patterns of behavior, process your emotions, and build strategies for navigating future relationships. Therapy provides a framework for personal growth, self-discovery, and healing.

Furthermore, self-care is paramount. Leaving a toxic relationship is emotionally draining, requiring substantial energy and resilience. Prioritize self-care practices that nurture your emotional and physical well-being. This might involve engaging in activities that bring you joy, such as spending time in nature, pursuing hobbies, or connecting with supportive friends. Prioritize healthy eating, regular exercise, and adequate sleep. These practices help restore your energy, boost your mood, and increase your resilience during the challenging process of healing.

It is important to remember that the healing process is not linear. There will be ups and downs, moments of progress, and periods of setbacks. Allow yourself to feel your emotions fully, without judgment or self-criticism. Avoid self-blame; remember that you are not responsible for the toxicity in the relationship. Acknowledge your feelings, process them healthily, and remember that healing is a journey that requires patience, self-compassion, and a steadfast commitment to your well-being.

Learning to recognize the signs of toxicity is not just about leaving a single relationship, it's about building healthier relationships in the future. It's about recognizing your worth, setting firm boundaries, and prioritizing your well-being. By understanding the dynamics of toxic relationships, you are empowering yourself to make informed choices that prioritize your happiness and fulfillment.

The path to freedom is often challenging, but the rewards are immense. Leaving a toxic relationship is an act of self-love, a commitment to building a life characterized by respect, dignity, and authentic connection. It's a journey of self-discovery, resilience, and empowerment, leading to a future filled with healthier, more fulfilling relationships and a renewed sense of self-worth. Embrace the strength within yourself, celebrate your progress, and remember that you deserve a life free from negativity and emotional manipulation. The path to healing may be arduous, but the journey to self-liberation is profoundly rewarding. The strength you demonstrate in leaving a toxic relationship is a testament to your resilience and a robust foundation for building a brighter future.

Embracing Acceptance

Embracing acceptance isn't about surrendering to defeat, it's about strategically allocating your energy. It's about recognizing that some things, despite our best efforts, remain beyond our control. This isn't resignation, it's a conscious choice to focus your resources where they can make a tangible difference. Think of it like a military strategist deploying troops: you wouldn't send your entire army to defend a position already lost, would you? You'd prioritize defending the territories that are still within your reach. Similarly, in life, acceptance helps you focus your energy on the battles you can win.

The act of accepting what cannot be changed isn't passive, it's powerfully active. It's about acknowledging reality, however harsh, and then deciding how you'll respond. This isn't about ignoring problems or pretending they don't exist, it's about recognizing their presence and deciding to approach them strategically. For example, you can't change the past, but you can learn from past mistakes and use that wisdom to guide future decisions. You can't control the weather, but you can prepare for a storm by having an emergency plan in place. You can't force someone to love you, but you can choose to love and respect yourself.

Many confuse acceptance with resignation. Resignation is passive, giving up without effort. Acceptance, on the other hand, is active, a recognition of reality that fuels proactive engagement with what is within your control. Resignation whispers, "There's nothing I can do," while acceptance declares, "This is what is, now let's figure out how to move forward." One leads to stagnation, the other to progress. Consider a person grieving a loss. Resignation might look like withdrawing from life entirely, shutting down emotionally, and refusing to engage with the world. Acceptance, however, involves acknowledging the pain of the loss while simultaneously making a conscious effort to honor the memory of the loved one by living a fulfilling life.

Let's delve into the practical aspects of embracing acceptance. One powerful tool is mindfulness. Mindfulness encourages us to observe our thoughts and feelings without judgment, acknowledging them without being overwhelmed by them. When faced with an unchangeable situation, instead of fighting against it, we can practice mindful observation. This doesn't mean condoning the situation, it means accepting its existence as a fact and then moving towards strategizing on what steps you can take to manage it effectively and minimize its negative impact on your life. For example, if you're dealing with a chronic illness, mindfulness could involve acknowledging the physical limitations and then focusing on creating a lifestyle that maximizes your capabilities while minimizing pain and discomfort.

Journaling can be another invaluable tool. Writing down your thoughts and feelings about a situation you're struggling to accept can help you process them more effectively. The act of writing can bring clarity and perspective. It allows you to externalize your emotions, giving you a more detached view. You might start by writing down everything you're feeling about the unchangeable situation: frustration, anger, sadness, grief. Then, try to shift your focus toward identifying what you can control. What actions can you take to alleviate some of the pressure and make the situation more manageable? For example, if you're facing financial hardship, you could write about your feelings of anxiety and desperation. Then, you can move towards listing concrete steps you can take, such as creating a budget, seeking financial advice, or exploring additional income streams.

Self-compassion is crucial in the journey of acceptance. Be kind to yourself. Recognize that it's okay to feel pain, anger, or frustration when faced with difficult circumstances. Don't beat yourself up for having these emotions. It's natural to struggle with acceptance. Give yourself time and space to process your feelings. Remember that embracing acceptance is not a one-time event but rather an ongoing process. There will be days when you falter, when you feel the pull of resistance. That's okay. Acknowledge these feelings without judgment, and gently redirect your focus back to the path of acceptance and proactive action.

The concept of acceptance extends beyond personal challenges to encompass broader societal issues. We can't change the prejudices that exist in the world, but we can actively challenge them, speak out against injustice, and work towards creating a more inclusive and equitable society. We can't control global warming, but we can make conscious efforts to reduce our carbon footprint and support sustainable practices. Acceptance here involves recognizing the reality of these situations while remaining actively engaged in creating positive change.

Acceptance doesn't imply passivity, it fuels action. Once you've accepted what you cannot change, you can shift your focus to what you can change, your response to the situation. This involves identifying actionable steps that will mitigate the negative impact, improve your well-being, and help you progress. For instance, if you've accepted that a toxic relationship is over, you can focus on healing, self-care, and building a healthy support network. If you've accepted the limitations of a physical disability, you can focus on adaptive strategies and assistive technologies that enhance your independence and quality of life.

It's vital to understand that acceptance is not a destination but a continuous process. There will be moments of doubt, setbacks, and even regression. The key is to recognize these moments as part of the journey, not as failures. Practice self-compassion, remind yourself of your progress, and refocus on the steps you can take to move forward. Celebrate small victories, acknowledge your resilience, and continue practicing acceptance as a daily tool in navigating life's challenges. The ability to accept what you cannot change is not a sign of weakness but a powerful strategy for building resilience, promoting well-being, and achieving lasting personal growth. This ability to distinguish between what is within and beyond your control, and to respond accordingly, is a hallmark of emotional maturity and a cornerstone of a fulfilling life.

Acceptance provides a foundation for forgiveness, a crucial step in letting go. Holding onto resentment and anger consumes energy and prevents progress. Forgiving others and, even more importantly, forgiving yourself opens the door to healing and peace. This doesn't mean condoning hurtful behavior, it means releasing the emotional burden it places on you and freeing yourself to move forward. Forgiveness allows you to release the past and embrace the present. It's an act of self-liberation, allowing you to reclaim your emotional energy and focus it on building a brighter future. It is an act of self-compassion, recognizing your human fallibility and extending that same grace to others.

The journey towards acceptance and forgiveness isn't always easy. It requires self-awareness, patience, and self-compassion. There will be days when you feel overwhelmed, and that is entirely understandable. But remember that even on the most challenging days, you can take small steps forward, and that's enough. The process of acceptance and forgiveness is a testament to your strength and your capacity for growth, a journey that empowers you to navigate life's challenges with resilience and grace, ultimately leading to a more peaceful and fulfilling life. The ability to accept and forgive is a powerful tool in your personal growth toolkit, a crucial step towards navigating life's inevitable hardships and creating a life defined by peace, contentment, and fulfillment. It is a continuous process, one that requires patience, self-compassion, and an unwavering commitment to your well-being. Embrace this journey, the rewards are profound.

Identifying Your Values

"When your values are clear to you, making decisions becomes easier."

Roy E. Disney

Identifying your core values is akin to creating a personal compass, guiding you through life's intricate maze of choices and uncertainties. These values, deeply held beliefs that shape your priorities and decisions, are the bedrock upon which a fulfilling and purposeful life is built. Without a clear understanding of your values, you risk drifting aimlessly, making choices that contradict your inner compass, and experiencing dissatisfaction and a sense of being unfulfilled.

This process of self-discovery is not a quick fix; it's a journey of introspection and self-reflection. It requires honesty, courage, and a willingness to confront your own beliefs and priorities. Many people go through life without ever consciously identifying their values, operating on autopilot and driven by external pressures rather than internal conviction. This often leads to a feeling of disconnect, a sense that something is missing despite outward successes. By consciously identifying your values, you take control of your life, aligning your actions with your beliefs, and cultivating a greater sense of authenticity and fulfillment.

One effective method for identifying your values is to reflect on moments of profound satisfaction or deep disappointment. Think back to times when you felt genuinely happy, fulfilled, or proud. What were you doing? What qualities or principles were in play? Analyze these experiences, searching for common threads that connect these moments of joy and accomplishment. These common threads often represent your core values. Conversely, review the times when you felt deeply disappointed or frustrated. What aspects of these experiences left you feeling disheartened? Understanding what you dislike can be just as illuminating as understanding what you love, as it often highlights values you hold dear that were violated or disregarded in those situations.

Another helpful technique is to consider the people you admire most. What qualities do these individuals possess that you respect and aspire to emulate? Their characteristics often reflect values that resonate with you. These could be qualities such as integrity, kindness, creativity, or perseverance. Identifying the traits you most admire in others can offer valuable insights into your value system. Remember to look beyond superficial attributes and explore the deeper principles that guide their behavior.

A powerful exercise is to create a list of potential values. Brainstorm a wide range of possibilities, from family and relationships to creativity, adventure, learning, and service. Don't censor yourself at this stage; jot down any value that comes to mind, no matter how seemingly insignificant it may appear. Once you have a comprehensive list, review each value, asking yourself how important it is to you on a scale of one to ten. This ranking will help you prioritize your values, differentiating between those that are fundamental to your being and those that are less central to your life.

Once you have prioritized your values, consider how these values are reflected, or not reflected, in your daily life. Are your choices and actions aligned with your core values? If not, where are the discrepancies? Identifying these areas of incongruence is crucial for making positive changes. This could involve re-evaluating your current commitments, career path, relationships, or lifestyle choices. This process requires courage, as it may involve making difficult decisions or altering aspects of your life that no longer resonate with your deepest values.

Visualizing your ideal future can also be a powerful tool. Imagine yourself five or ten years from now, living a life that is wholly aligned with your values. What does that life look like? What are you doing? Who are you with? This visualization exercise can provide a clearer picture of the life you want to create and the steps you need to take to get there. It allows you to connect your values with your aspirations, offering a concrete roadmap for achieving your goals.

It's important to remember that values are not static; they can evolve as you grow and change. Regularly reviewing and reflecting on your values is crucial to ensure your life remains aligned with your deepest beliefs. Life experiences, personal growth, and shifting circumstances can all influence your value system. Embrace this dynamism. It is a sign of growth and evolution, not a weakness. Revisit this exercise from time to time, allowing yourself to reassess your values as you navigate life's journey.

Another beneficial exercise involves identifying your "non-negotiables." These are the values so fundamental to your being that you would never compromise them, regardless of the situation. These might include honesty, integrity, or kindness. Understanding your non-negotiables can provide a strong moral compass, helping you navigate difficult decisions with clarity and conviction. Knowing your limits and boundaries empowers you to say no to opportunities or situations that conflict with these deeply held principles, preserving your integrity and sense of self.

Consider how your values align with those of your close friends and family. Surrounding yourself with people who share similar values can foster supportive and enriching relationships. However, differences in values are inevitable and often provide valuable learning opportunities. Understanding these differences can lead to greater empathy and tolerance, strengthening relationships based on mutual respect. Still, if significant and irreconcilable value conflicts exist, it may be necessary to re-evaluate the health and compatibility of those relationships.

Journaling can provide an invaluable resource throughout this process. Use your journal to capture your thoughts, feelings, and insights as you work through the exercises outlined here. Journaling offers a safe space for introspection, allowing you to delve deeply into your beliefs and priorities without judgment. Regularly reviewing your entries can help you recognize patterns or shifts in your value system. It becomes a living document of your personal growth and evolution.

Identifying your core values is not a passive activity. It is an ongoing process of self-discovery that requires intention, effort, and honest reflection. Yet the rewards are immense. By understanding your values, you gain clarity about what truly matters to you, giving you a reliable compass for making life choices that lead to fulfillment and meaning. It's the foundation for building a life that aligns with your deepest beliefs and aspirations, ultimately leading to greater well-being and inner peace. Embrace this journey of self-discovery. The insights you uncover will transform your life in profound ways. This process will not only help you make better decisions but will also deepen your self-awareness and support a more authentic, purpose-driven life. It is an investment in yourself, a pledge to live intentionally and meaningfully, guided by the wisdom of your values.

Exploring Your Interests and Talents

> *"Don't ask yourself what the world needs. Ask yourself what makes you come alive, and go do that. Because what the world needs is people who have come alive."*
>
> Howard Thurman

Having established a strong foundation by identifying your core values, we now turn our attention to exploring the vibrant landscape of your interests, passions, and talents. This is a crucial step in the journey toward finding your purpose and passion because understanding your aptitudes and inclinations provides a roadmap for aligning your actions with your deepest values. It's not just about what you should do; it's about discovering what you love to do and how you can leverage your abilities to create a life of meaning and fulfillment.

This exploration is not simply about listing hobbies; it's a deeper dive into your intrinsic motivations and capabilities. Think of it as an archaeological expedition into your psyche, unearthing buried treasures of potential and passion. It's a process of self-discovery that requires honest self-reflection, a willingness to experiment, and a commitment to embracing the unknown.

One effective technique is to revisit your childhood. What activities did you find yourself gravitating towards? What ignited your imagination and kept you engrossed for hours? Often, the passions that fueled our youthful enthusiasm are still present, perhaps dormant, waiting to be rekindled. Consider the games you played, the books you read, the creative projects you undertook. These early experiences often provide clues about your inherent talents and interests. Did you spend hours building elaborate Lego castles? This might suggest an aptitude for architecture or engineering. Were you a voracious reader, lost in fantastical worlds? This could hint at a passion for storytelling or writing. Reconnect with those moments of pure joy and engagement; they hold valuable insights into your natural inclinations.

Beyond childhood, consider your present-day activities. What tasks do you find yourself effortlessly engrossed in? What projects make you lose track of time? These spontaneous moments of deep engagement often reveal hidden talents and unexplored passions. Even seemingly mundane tasks can offer clues. You may find immense satisfaction in organizing your closet, hinting at a potential for meticulous work or interior design. Or you may derive pleasure from cooking elaborate meals, suggesting a potential for culinary arts. Pay attention to the small moments of joy and flow. They are the signposts pointing toward your path.

Another crucial aspect of this exploration is identifying your talents. These are the skills and abilities you possess, honed through experience and practice. Talents are not necessarily innate gifts; they are often developed through dedicated effort and persistent learning. However, you might find that specific skills come more naturally to you than others, requiring less effort to master. Identifying these natural aptitudes can help you focus your energy on areas where you have a comparative advantage, maximizing your potential for success and fulfillment.

To identify your talents, seek feedback from trusted friends, family members, and colleagues. Ask for their honest assessments of your strengths and abilities. Their perspectives can often illuminate aspects of yourself that you might have overlooked. Pay close attention to recurring themes or patterns in the feedback you receive. This input can also help you uncover any blind spots and highlight areas where you may underestimate your abilities or lack confidence.

In addition to seeking external feedback, consider engaging in self-assessment exercises. There are many well-regarded online tools and personality assessments that can offer insights into your strengths, preferences, and areas for growth. While these tools should not be viewed as definitive labels, they can serve as valuable starting points for reflection. Use them as one piece of a larger self-exploration process, blending their suggestions with your own personal insights and lived experiences.

Once you've gathered ideas about your interests and strengths, take time to reflect on how they might intersect or support one another. Often, a deeply fulfilling life path doesn't come from a single skill or passion, but from a unique combination of several. Try visualizing this as a Venn diagram, with different circles representing your talents, interests, and values. The space where they overlap may point to meaningful and enriching directions that are uniquely suited to you.

For example, if you have a strong interest in writing and a natural ease with public speaking, you might consider opportunities in journalism, education, or even advocacy. Or, if you enjoy helping others and have strong planning skills, careers in counseling or nonprofit project management might be a good fit. When you explore how your different abilities and passions work together, you open yourself up to new possibilities you may not have previously imagined.

It's equally important to remain open to exploration. Self-discovery is not always straightforward. It often involves trying new things, adjusting your course, and learning from experience. Step outside your comfort zone, and allow space for missteps. Even failure can be incredibly instructive. It teaches resilience, provides clarity, and often reveals insights about what truly brings you joy and meaning.

Throughout this journey, keep curiosity at the forefront. Let your interests evolve as you grow. It's normal for passions to shift over time, especially as you gain new experiences. The process of exploring your potential should remain flexible and responsive. What matters most is staying connected to what feels authentic and engaging, and being willing to adjust course when needed. Each new insight brings you closer to a life that aligns with your deeper self.

Finally, always return to your values as your anchor. No matter how exciting a talent or interest may seem, if it conflicts with what matters most to you, it is unlikely to bring lasting satisfaction. The true sweet spot is found where your values, interests, and talents converge. That is where your energy will feel sustainable, your effort will feel worthwhile, and your path will feel aligned. You don't have to rush. This journey of discovery takes time, but it leads to a life built on clarity, authenticity, and deep personal fulfillment.

Setting Meaningful Goals

"You are never too old to set another goal or to dream a new dream."

C.S. Lewis

Now that you've delved into the rich tapestry of your values, interests, and talents, it's time to translate these discoveries into actionable steps. This means setting meaningful goals that are not simply arbitrary checkpoints but intentional milestones along your path to a purposeful and fulfilling life. This is the moment where clarity meets action, where self-discovery becomes movement, and where your insights begin to shape your future in tangible ways.

The key to setting meaningful goals lies in aligning them with your intrinsic motivation. While external rewards like money, recognition, or status can provide temporary encouragement, they rarely fuel sustained progress. Enduring fulfillment comes from goals that are rooted in your values and passions, the kinds of goals that excite you and give your efforts deeper significance. These are the pursuits you commit to not because you are expected to, but because they feel personally important and energizing.

Consider this: setting a goal to earn a million dollars might sound impressive, but without deeper meaning, it can feel hollow. If, however, that money represents the freedom to travel and document environmental issues or the ability to support a community initiative that aligns with your values, then it becomes a vessel for impact. In this context, the goal gains substance.

It shifts from being an arbitrary number to a symbol of your desire to contribute meaningfully to the world around you.

Setting meaningful goals is not a one-time act; it's an evolving process. As you grow, so will your priorities, and your goals should reflect those changes. Adaptability is essential. Clinging to outdated goals out of habit or fear can lead to stagnation. Instead, make it a regular practice to revisit your intentions, reflect on your current reality, and refine your goals accordingly. This fluid approach ensures that your efforts remain in harmony with your values and evolving vision, keeping you motivated and aligned over time.

To begin, let's explore a framework for setting practical goals. The SMART framework provides a proper structure:

Specific: Your goals should be clearly defined and unambiguous. Instead of setting a vague goal like "improve my health," aim for something specific, such as "walk for 30 minutes three times a week." The more precise your goals, the easier it will be to track your progress and measure your success.

Measurable: Incorporate quantifiable metrics into your goals. This practice allows you to track your progress objectively and celebrate your achievements along the way. Instead of "learn a new language," aim to "learn 500 vocabulary words and be able to hold a basic conversation in Spanish within six months."

Achievable: While it's essential to challenge yourself, your goals should also be realistic and attainable. Setting overly ambitious goals can lead to discouragement and ultimately derail your progress. Start with smaller, manageable steps that would build momentum and confidence.

Relevant: Please make sure that your goals align with your values, passions, and overall life vision. This is crucial for maintaining intrinsic motivation. Goals that feel irrelevant or forced will likely be abandoned before they are completed.

Time-bound: Set deadlines for your goals to create a sense of urgency and accountability. This practice helps to prevent procrastination and keeps you focused on making consistent progress. Instead of "write a novel," aim for "write a chapter of my novel every week for the next year."

However, the SMART framework alone isn't sufficient. Meaningful goals go beyond simple task completion; they encompass a sense of purpose and contribution. Please take into account the impact your goals will have on yourself and others. How will achieving these goals contribute to your personal growth, your relationships, or your community? Reflecting on the broader implications of your goals makes it more critical and reinforces your commitment.

Consider breaking down larger, overarching goals into smaller, more manageable sub-goals. This creates a sense of accomplishment as you achieve each milestone, keeping you motivated and preventing feelings of being overwhelmed. Visualizing your progress, using a chart or a planner, can reinforce this sense of achievement.

Furthermore, it's crucial to anticipate potential obstacles and develop strategies for overcoming them. Life is unpredictable, and setbacks are inevitable. By proactively identifying potential challenges and creating contingency plans, you increase your resilience and your chances of success. This doesn't mean eliminating all risks, it means approaching challenges with a proactive mindset, viewing them as opportunities for growth and learning.

Remember, the journey towards achieving your goals is as important as the destination. Embrace the process, celebrate your successes (no matter how small), and learn from your setbacks. Maintain a growth mindset, viewing challenges as opportunities for learning and development rather than indicators of failure. Self-compassion is essential, be kind to yourself during the process, acknowledging that progress is rarely linear.

Beyond the SMART framework, consider incorporating visualization techniques. Regularly visualizing yourself achieving your goals can significantly enhance your motivation and commitment. Imagine yourself experiencing the satisfaction and fulfillment that comes with achieving your aspirations. This mental rehearsal strengthens your commitment and makes your goals feel more tangible and achievable.

Incorporating affirmations can also bolster your motivation. Regularly repeating positive statements about your abilities and your capacity to achieve your goals can reinforce your self-belief and confidence. These affirmations should be specific and personalized, reflecting your unique aspirations and strengths.

The process of goal setting is not merely about achieving specific outcomes, it's about cultivating a mindset of continuous growth and development. It's about fostering a sense of purpose and direction, aligning your actions with your deepest values and aspirations. It's about creating a life that is both meaningful and fulfilling.

Throughout this process, remember to stay connected to your core values. Regularly revisiting your values ensures that your goals remain aligned with your most profound sense of self, preventing you from pursuing goals that may ultimately lead to dissatisfaction. Maintain a journal to reflect on your progress, your challenges, and your evolving sense of purpose. This regular self-reflection is crucial for staying on track and making necessary adjustments along the way.

Don't be afraid to seek support from others. Sharing your goals with trusted friends, family, or mentors can provide accountability, encouragement, and valuable perspective. A supportive network can make all the difference in overcoming challenges and staying motivated.

Finally, celebrate your accomplishments. Acknowledge and appreciate your progress, no matter how small. This positive reinforcement is crucial for maintaining momentum and fostering a sense of self-efficacy. Be sure to reward yourself for your achievements, but make sure the rewards are aligned with your overall goals and values. This positive feedback loop will keep you motivated and engaged in the process.

Setting meaningful goals is a journey of self-discovery and personal growth. It's a dynamic process requiring flexibility, adaptability, and a commitment to continuous self-reflection. Embrace the challenges, celebrate the victories, and remember that the journey itself is a testament to your resilience and determination. The path may be winding, but the destination, a life of purpose and passion, is worth the effort. The journey is not merely about reaching a destination, it's about becoming the person capable of achieving your dreams. And that, in itself, is a profoundly rewarding experience.

Overcoming Fear and Self-Doubt

> *"Our doubts are traitors, and make us lose the good we oft might win, by fearing to attempt."*
>
> Willliam Shakespeare, Measure for Measure

The journey toward discovering and living a life fueled by purpose and passion is rarely a smooth, uninterrupted ascent. It's more akin to navigating a winding mountain trail, replete with challenging inclines, unexpected detours, and moments where the sheer scale of the undertaking can feel overwhelming. One of the most significant obstacles on this path is the internal landscape of fear and self-doubt. These insidious companions can whisper doubts, question your abilities, undermine your confidence, and ultimately paralyze you before you even begin.

This is a crucial juncture in our exploration of purpose and passion. The groundwork has been laid, you've identified your values, explored your interests, and defined meaningful goals. However, translating these aspirations into reality requires confronting the often-unseen barriers of fear and self-doubt. These internal adversaries are not inherently harmful, they are, in fact, survival mechanisms. Fear, at its core, is a warning signal, a protective instinct designed to keep us safe from perceived threats. Self-doubt, similarly, is a form of self-preservation, preventing us from venturing into territories where we might experience failure or disappointment.

The challenge lies not in eradicating fear and self-doubt, which is often unrealistic and even undesirable, but in learning to manage them, recognize them for what they are, and develop strategies to navigate their presence without letting them dictate your actions. Think of fear and self-doubt as the shadows that accompany the light of your aspirations. While they may obscure the path at times, they don't have to extinguish your inner flame.

One powerful strategy for overcoming fear is to confront it directly rather than avoiding it. This involves actively stepping into situations that evoke fear, even if it's just a tiny, incremental step. This process of gradual exposure, known in psychology as desensitization, helps to reduce the intensity of your fear response over time. Consider, for example, someone who has a fear of public speaking. Instead of trying to conquer their fear all at once by giving a large presentation, they might start by speaking to a small group of friends, then a slightly larger group, and gradually increase the size of the audience until they feel comfortable speaking in front of a larger gathering.

The power of small steps cannot be overstated. It's not about grand gestures or dramatic leaps, it's about consistent, incremental progress. Each small victory builds confidence, creating a positive feedback loop that fuels further progress. This is especially important when dealing with deeply ingrained fears or self-doubts. Celebrating these small wins is crucial, creating a sense of accomplishment and bolstering self-esteem. A small win might be something as simple as writing a single paragraph of a book chapter or having a short conversation with a stranger when you usually avoid such interactions.

Another effective strategy is to reframe your thinking. Often, our fears are based on catastrophic thinking, imagining the worst-case scenario without considering more likely, less adverse outcomes. Challenging these negative thoughts and replacing them with more realistic and positive ones is a powerful way to reduce anxiety and increase confidence. For example, instead of thinking, "I'm going to fail this presentation, and everyone will laugh at me," try reframing the thought as, "I've prepared well, and even if I make a few mistakes, it's an opportunity to learn and grow."

Self-compassion is an invaluable tool in this journey. Be kind to yourself, acknowledge that setbacks and failures are a normal part of the learning process. Please don't beat yourself up over mistakes, instead, learn from them and move forward. Treat yourself with the same kindness and understanding that you would offer a close friend facing similar challenges. Remember that progress is rarely linear, there will be ups and downs, moments of doubt, and moments of clarity. Self-compassion allows you to navigate these fluctuations with grace and resilience.

Visualizing success can be surprisingly effective in reducing fear and self-doubt. Spend time regularly imagining yourself achieving your goals, experiencing feelings of satisfaction and accomplishment. This mental rehearsal builds confidence and helps you to anticipate and overcome potential obstacles, the more vivid and realistic your visualizations, the more powerful their effect.

Building a strong support network is also crucial. Surrounding yourself with people who believe in you and who offer encouragement and support can significantly boost your confidence and resilience. Share your goals and aspirations with trusted friends, family members, or mentors, their belief in your abilities can be a powerful antidote to self-doubt. They can offer valuable perspective, support during challenging times, and celebrate your successes.

Consider the example of Amelia Earhart, a pioneer aviator who faced immense fear and self-doubt throughout her career. Her solo flights across the Atlantic and the Pacific were not merely feats of daring, they were triumphs over her internal struggles. Her perseverance in the face of adversity serves as an inspiring example of the power of courage and determination. She didn't let her fears prevent her from pursuing her dreams, and neither should you.

Or consider Malala Yousafzai, who, despite facing the risk of death, fought tirelessly for the right of girls to receive an education. Her courage in the face of overwhelming fear exemplifies the profound impact that can be achieved when one overcomes self-doubt and acts in accordance with one's convictions. Her story underscores the fact that the most significant risks often yield the greatest rewards.

Remember that the discomfort you feel when stepping outside your comfort zone is a sign that you are growing. It's a signal that you're challenging yourself, pushing your boundaries, and expanding your capabilities. Embrace this discomfort, view it as an indicator of progress, a testament to your courage and resilience. Growth doesn't occur in comfortable spaces, it's forged in the crucible of challenge and uncertainty.

Finally, remember that your purpose and passion are not fixed, static entities, they are dynamic, evolving forces. Allow yourself the freedom to explore, to experiment, and to change course as needed. The journey towards discovering and living a purposeful and passionate life is a lifelong process, not a destination. Embrace the uncertainties, the detours, and the inevitable setbacks. Learn from them, grow from them, and continue to move forward, one step at a time.

The path may be unpredictable, but the destination, a life of meaning and fulfillment, is well worth the effort. And the person you become during the journey, resilient and courageous, is the greatest reward of all. The ability to conquer fear and self-doubt is not an innate quality, it's a skill developed through consistent effort and self-reflection. It's a journey of continuous growth and self-discovery, one that's both challenging and profoundly rewarding. Embrace the process, celebrate the small victories, and remember that you are capable of far more than you might believe.

Creating a Life of Purpose

"The meaning of life is to find your gift. The purpose of life is to give it away."

Pablo Picasso

Having conquered the internal landscape of fear and self-doubt, the next crucial step is to actively create a life that reflects your discovered purpose and passion. This isn't a passive process, it requires conscious effort, consistent action, and a willingness to adapt and adjust along the way. Think of it as building a house: you've laid the foundation (identified your values and goals), and now it's time to construct the walls, install the roof, and furnish the interior, all while ensuring the structure remains aligned with your initial blueprint.

The first step towards creating a life of purpose involves integrating your values and passions into your daily routines. This might involve setting aside dedicated time each day for activities that align with your core values. If, for example, your core value is connection, schedule regular time for meaningful conversations with loved ones, volunteer in your community, or join a social group. If your passion lies in creativity, dedicate an hour each morning to painting, writing, or playing music. This consistent engagement, even in small doses, reinforces your values and fuels your passion, turning them from abstract ideals into tangible realities.

Consider the concept of "micro-actions." These are small, manageable actions that contribute to your larger goals. They're the building blocks of a purposeful life. Instead of feeling overwhelmed by the prospect of writing a novel, start by writing a single paragraph each day. Instead of aiming for a marathon, start with a daily walk. These small, consistent actions, seemingly insignificant on their own, compound over time to create substantial progress. They also cultivate a sense of accomplishment and momentum, preventing you from succumbing to inertia or discouragement.

Another powerful technique is to incorporate your values and passions into your professional life. This might involve seeking out opportunities for professional development that align with your interests or actively seeking out a career that allows you to utilize your skills and talents in a meaningful way. This isn't necessarily about a complete career overhaul, it might involve taking on new responsibilities within your current role or seeking out opportunities for mentorship or training that expand your skillset and allow you to contribute more effectively to your organization. A fulfilling career isn't just about financial stability, it's about contributing to something larger than yourself and feeling a sense of purpose and accomplishment in your work.

Setting long-term goals is essential for creating a life of purpose. These goals provide direction and motivation, guiding your actions and decisions. However, these goals shouldn't be rigid, unyielding targets, they should be flexible and adaptable, allowing for course correction as you learn and grow. The process of setting goals should be a continuous, iterative process involving regular reflection and adjustment as your values, priorities, and circumstances change over time. It's a dynamic process, not a static one.

Regular self-reflection is paramount in this journey. It's through consistent self-examination that we identify areas of alignment and misalignment between our actions and our values. Please don't hesitate to set aside time each week or month to reflect on your progress, challenges, and areas for improvement. Journaling, meditation, or simply engaging in quiet contemplation can provide valuable insights into your internal landscape and help you identify areas where you might need to adjust your course.

One method for self-reflection is to ask yourself powerful questions: "Am I living in alignment with my values?" "Are my actions contributing to my long-term goals?" "What obstacles are preventing me from progressing, and how can I overcome them?" "What am I grateful for?" Honest answers to these questions can reveal subtle shifts in your values or priorities, allowing you to adjust your course accordingly.

Another critical aspect of creating a life of purpose is cultivating a mindset of gratitude. Practicing gratitude helps to shift your focus from what's lacking in your life to what's abundant. It fosters a sense of contentment and appreciation, increasing overall well-being and resilience. Take time each day to reflect on the things you're grateful for, no matter how small they may seem. A simple act of expressing gratitude can shift your perspective and increase your sense of purpose.

Furthermore, remember that creating a life of purpose is not a solo endeavor. Surround yourself with a supportive community of like-minded individuals who share your values and passions. These individuals can provide encouragement, support, and accountability as you navigate the challenges and setbacks that inevitably arise. They can offer valuable perspective, celebrate your successes, and provide a sense of belonging and connection.

Building a strong support system is crucial. This may involve joining a professional organization, participating in a hobby group, or cultivating deeper relationships with close friends and family. These relationships provide a sense of belonging, encouragement, and a network of support during challenging times. They can provide a sounding board for your ideas, offer valuable insights, and celebrate your successes.

Remember that your purpose and passion are not fixed entities, they're dynamic, evolving forces that will change over time. Allow yourself the flexibility to explore different paths, experiment with new ideas, and adapt your approach as you learn and grow. The journey of discovering and living a life of purpose is a continuous process of self-discovery and refinement.

Embrace the inevitable setbacks and challenges that will arise along the way. They are not roadblocks, they are opportunities for learning and growth. View them as valuable lessons that will help you to refine your approach and to deepen your understanding of yourself and your purpose. They are integral to the process, shaping your resilience and strengthening your commitment.

Finally, remember that creating a life of purpose is a marathon, not a sprint. It requires consistent effort, unwavering dedication, and a willingness to adapt and adjust along the way. Celebrate your successes, both big and small, and learn from your mistakes. With consistent effort and self-reflection, you can create a life that is both purposeful and fulfilling, a life that is truly your own. The journey itself is a testament to your growth and resilience, a testament to your ability to overcome obstacles and create a life that aligns with your values and passions. The fulfillment you gain from this process, the continuous striving, the overcoming of challenges, and the feeling of living authentically is a reward in itself, far exceeding any single achievement. This journey of self-discovery is lifelong, embrace the continuous evolution of your purpose and passion, allowing yourself to adapt and grow with the ever-changing landscape of your life.

Building Self-Discipline

"Discipline is the bridge between goals and accomplishment."

Jim Rohn

Building self-discipline is not about superhuman willpower, it's about strategically designing your environment and habits to support your goals. It's about understanding your brain's tendencies and working with them, not against them. Think of self-discipline not as a muscle you magically strengthen overnight but as a skill you meticulously hone over time. The journey requires patience, self-compassion, and a willingness to experiment with different strategies until you find what resonates with you.

One highly effective strategy involves the power of small, consistent actions. Instead of aiming for drastic, overwhelming changes, focus on making incremental improvements. This approach, often referred to as "kaizen," emphasizes continuous, incremental progress. Instead of vowing to exercise for two hours daily, a goal that's quickly abandoned, commit to just ten minutes. This small, achievable goal is less intimidating, fostering a sense of accomplishment that motivates you to continue. Gradually increase the duration as your discipline grows. This approach applies to any area of life: learning a new language by studying five words a day, writing a book one paragraph at a time, or improving your diet by making one healthier meal swap per day. These micro-wins build momentum, fueling your motivation and solidifying the habit.

Habit formation is a crucial aspect of building self-discipline. Habits are automated behaviors and ingrained responses that require minimal conscious effort. This automation is key to sustaining positive change. Consider the science behind habit formation, often described as a "habit loop," which consists of a cue that triggers the behavior, a routine which is the behavior itself, and a reward that reinforces the habit. To build a new habit, identify your cue, design a simple routine, and provide yourself with a satisfying reward. For example, if your goal is to read more, your cue could be finishing your evening tea, the routine could be reading for fifteen minutes, and the reward might be a feeling of relaxation and accomplishment. The more consistent you are with this loop, the stronger the habit becomes.

Another powerful technique involves leveraging the power of accountability. Sharing your goals with someone you trust, whether a friend, family member, or coach, can significantly increase your chances of success. Knowing that someone else is aware of your commitment adds an extra layer of motivation, making you more likely to follow through. This accountability can take many forms, including regular check-ins, shared progress reports, or even a friendly competition. Consider joining a group or community focused on your goal. The shared experience, mutual encouragement, and sense of belonging can be invaluable in maintaining momentum. A supportive environment makes a real difference in overcoming moments of doubt or discouragement.

Environmental design plays a surprisingly significant role in self-discipline. Your surroundings have a powerful influence on your behavior. If your goal is to improve your health, remove tempting junk food from your home. If your goal is to read more, create a cozy reading space. Strategically organizing your environment helps reduce distractions and increases the likelihood of engaging in your chosen behavior. This also applies to your digital space: turn off unnecessary notifications, use website blockers, and curate your social media to support your focus. A well-designed environment supports your efforts subtly and effectively by making positive actions easier and negative ones more difficult.

Self-compassion is crucial to the process. Building self-discipline is not a straight path, it involves setbacks and occasional failures. Know that mistakes are part of the journey and offer important learning opportunities. Practice self-forgiveness, and remind yourself that imperfection is part of being human. Instead of giving up after missing a workout or breaking a commitment, choose to realign with your goals. Gently recommit and move forward. This mindset keeps you motivated and helps you maintain your momentum, especially during difficult periods.

Time management techniques can significantly enhance your self-discipline. Prioritize your tasks, assigning specific times for the ones most critical to your goals. Explore time-blocking, where you dedicate blocks of time to specific activities. This structure provides clarity, reduces distractions, and brings a sense of order to your day. Learn to say "no" to commitments that don't serve your priorities. Protect your time and energy for the things that matter most. Effective time management isn't about doing more, it's about doing what aligns with your values and long-term vision. This focused approach sustains discipline and helps you stay aligned with what truly matters.

Visualization is a powerful tool for strengthening self-discipline. Regularly visualize yourself achieving your goals and imagine the feelings of accomplishment and satisfaction. This mental rehearsal strengthens your commitment and reinforces your belief in your ability to succeed. You can create a vision board representing your goals and review it regularly as a reminder of your aspirations. By mentally preparing for success, you build confidence and resilience, increasing your motivation to overcome obstacles.

Mindfulness practices, such as meditation or deep breathing exercises, can enhance self-discipline by improving your ability to focus and manage impulses. These techniques help you become more aware of your thoughts and emotions, enabling you to respond to situations rather than react impulsively. Mindfulness promotes emotional regulation, increasing your ability to stay calm and focused in the face of challenges. Regular mindfulness practice builds mental strength, enhancing your capacity for self-control. It's a valuable tool for managing cravings and resisting distractions.

Finally, celebrate your progress. Acknowledge and appreciate your achievements, both big and small. Recognize the effort you've invested and the obstacles you've overcome. These celebrations, however small, are crucial for maintaining motivation and preventing burnout. Take time to reflect on how far you've come and appreciate the positive changes you've made. This positive reinforcement strengthens your commitment and encourages you to continue your journey. Remember that building self-discipline is a marathon, not a sprint, so celebrate each milestone along the way. Your dedication, commitment, and persistence are what ultimately define success. The journey itself, with its triumphs and challenges, is a testament to your resilience and evolving capacity for self-mastery.

Celebrating Achievements

"Success is the sum of small efforts, repeated day in and day out."

Robert Collier

Celebrating achievements isn't about boasting or arrogance, it's about acknowledging the effort you've invested and reinforcing the positive feelings that fuel your continued progress. It's about recognizing the small victories that build towards more significant accomplishments. Many people struggle with this, as they tend to focus intensely on the end goal, overlooking the significant milestones achieved along the way. This can lead to burnout, discouragement, and, ultimately, giving up. The truth is that consistent forward movement is built upon a foundation of acknowledging and celebrating progress, no matter how seemingly insignificant.

Think about it: each small step forward, every challenge overcome, and every goal achieved, no matter how small, is a testament to your resilience and your unwavering commitment. These are achievements deserving of recognition and celebration. But how do you effectively celebrate your achievements? It's not just about throwing a party (though that can be fun), it's about cultivating a mindset that values and acknowledges your efforts.

One effective technique is to maintain a "success journal." This isn't a diary of your daily minutiae, it's a dedicated space to record your accomplishments, no matter how small. Did you finally finish that challenging project at work? Did you manage to resist that tempting dessert? Did you dedicate thirty minutes to exercise, exceeding your initial goal of fifteen? All of these deserve a place in your journal. Write them down, detailing not just the achievement itself but also the feelings associated with it. How did you feel when you completed that task? What emotions arose as a result of your accomplishment? This process strengthens the positive association with your efforts, making you more likely to repeat the behavior.

Beyond writing in a journal, create a visual representation of your progress. This could be a simple chart tracking your progress toward a larger goal, or it could be a more elaborate vision board showcasing your aspirations and achievements. Visualizing your progress provides a tangible reminder of how far you've come, fostering a sense of accomplishment and motivating you to continue. Seeing the tangible evidence of your efforts can be incredibly powerful in combating feelings of discouragement or self-doubt. The act of creating the visual aids itself is also a form of celebration, as it forces you to pause and reflect on your achievements.

Another powerful method involves sharing your accomplishments with others. This doesn't mean bragging, it's about seeking support and validation from trusted friends, family members, or mentors. Sharing your successes with others creates a sense of accountability and provides a platform for positive reinforcement. The act of sharing your progress can also generate further motivation, as you'll be more likely to maintain your momentum if you know others are aware of your progress.

Consider the power of small, regular celebrations. This doesn't require elaborate gestures, it could be something as simple as enjoying a favorite cup of tea after a productive workday, taking a relaxing bath after a challenging workout, or reading a chapter of your favorite book as a reward for achieving a milestone. These small acts of self-care serve as positive reinforcement, associating accomplishment with pleasant experiences. They help solidify the positive feelings connected to your efforts, reinforcing the behavior and encouraging repetition.

It's crucial to differentiate between celebration and reward. A reward is often something external, such as a material purchase or a special outing. While rewards can be motivating, they shouldn't be the primary focus of your celebration. The most potent celebrations are those that tap into your intrinsic motivation, acknowledging the internal sense of satisfaction and accomplishment you feel. External rewards can lose their effectiveness over time, whereas the intrinsic satisfaction of a job well done remains a powerful motivator.

It's also important to be mindful of the tendency to undervalue your accomplishments. Many people suffer from what's known as "imposter syndrome," where they downplay their successes, attributing them to luck or external factors. This self-deprecating behavior can undermine your efforts and hinder your motivation. Actively challenge this mindset. When you achieve something, take a moment to fully appreciate your role in its success. Acknowledge the skills, knowledge, and effort you invested. Give yourself credit for your hard work and dedication.

Another element often overlooked is self-compassion. Celebrating achievements doesn't mean ignoring setbacks. It means acknowledging both your successes and your failures with equal measure and understanding that progress isn't always linear. Setbacks are an inevitable part of any journey, and they shouldn't diminish the value of your accomplishments. Learn from your mistakes, adjust your approach, and continue moving forward. Celebrate the resilience you've demonstrated in overcoming obstacles. This balanced perspective promotes sustained motivation, allowing you to bounce back from adversity and continue celebrating your ongoing progress.

Furthermore, ensure your celebrations are authentic to you. Avoid feeling pressured to celebrate in ways that don't resonate with you. If public displays of achievement aren't your style, that's perfectly okay. The goal is to find ways to acknowledge your accomplishments that feel meaningful and rewarding to you. What genuinely makes you feel good? What activities foster a sense of accomplishment and well-being? Tailor your celebrations to your individual needs and preferences.

Finally, remember that celebrating your achievements is not selfish, it's essential for maintaining momentum and preventing burnout. It's about nurturing your intrinsic motivation, reinforcing positive feelings, and fostering a mindset that embraces both successes and setbacks. By acknowledging your efforts and celebrating your progress, you cultivate a more profound sense of self-belief and resilience, fueling your continued journey toward your goals. Celebrate your wins, learn from your losses, and keep moving forward. The journey is as important, if not more so, than the destination. Each step taken, each hurdle overcome, and each achievement reached is a testament to your strength and perseverance, a victory worthy of celebration. Embrace the journey, savor the successes, and continue to build upon your accomplishments. The process of consistent progress, fueled by self-acknowledgment and appreciation, is what truly defines your success.

Learning from Setbacks

Learning from setbacks is not about dwelling on failures, it's about extracting valuable lessons that propel us forward. It's a crucial element often overlooked in the pursuit of success. We celebrate achievements, rightfully so, but how we handle the inevitable stumbles dictates our long-term progress. A resilient spirit isn't forged in the absence of hardship, it's tempered by the way we navigate those challenges.

The first step in learning from setbacks is honest self-reflection. Avoid the temptation to blame external factors or minimize your role in the outcome. Ask yourself probing questions: What went wrong? Where did my strategy fall short? What could I have done differently? Were there warning signs I missed? This introspective process is not about self-flagellation, it's about gaining a clearer understanding of the situation and identifying areas for improvement.

Many people find it helpful to write down their thoughts and feelings after a setback. This can serve as a valuable tool for processing emotions and identifying patterns. The act of writing itself can be surprisingly therapeutic, allowing you to articulate your experience in a structured way rather than letting emotions overwhelm you. You can also use this written reflection to identify potential solutions or alternative approaches.

Consider keeping a dedicated "setback journal," similar to your success journal. This journal isn't a place to wallow in negativity, instead, it's a space to analyze challenges objectively, extract lessons, and formulate new strategies. Record the setback, your immediate emotional response, your analysis of contributing factors, and, most importantly, the steps you'll take to prevent similar situations in the future. This process transforms setbacks from obstacles into opportunities for growth and development.

Another crucial element is separating the event from your self-worth. Setbacks are not indicators of your overall capabilities or character. A failed project doesn't mean you're a failure, a missed deadline doesn't mean you're incompetent. These are isolated incidents, they do not define your entire being. Maintaining a healthy sense of self-esteem in the face of adversity is essential for your resilience and your ability to learn from the experience.

Remember the concept of progress over perfection. Setbacks are inevitable in any pursuit, they're part of the journey. The key is to keep moving forward despite the stumbles. Focus on continuous improvement, not flawlessness. Progress, however incremental, is still progress. Celebrate the small victories along the way, even as you learn from setbacks. This balanced perspective fosters a sense of accomplishment and prevents discouragement.

Let's delve into practical examples. Imagine an entrepreneur launching a new business. The initial marketing campaign falls flat, sales are below projections. Instead of succumbing to despair, the entrepreneur analyzes the campaign: Was the target audience correctly identified? Was the messaging effective? Were the marketing channels chosen appropriately? The entrepreneur may discover that the target audience was too narrowly defined or that the chosen advertising platform wasn't reaching the desired demographic. This analysis provides crucial insights for adjusting the marketing strategy in future campaigns. The setback becomes a learning experience, refining the approach and increasing the likelihood of future success.

Consider another scenario: an athlete preparing for a significant competition. They experience a setback during training, an injury that hinders their progress. This setback forces a reevaluation of their training regimen. They may need to adjust their workout intensity, incorporate physical therapy, or modify their training schedule. The athlete learns to listen to their body, prioritize recovery, and adjust their approach to training. The setback becomes an opportunity to strengthen their resilience and refine their training methods, ultimately leading to a more robust and sustainable approach to their athletic goals.

A common mistake is to avoid analyzing setbacks due to the emotional discomfort involved. This is a crucial error. Facing uncomfortable truths about our actions and their consequences is often painful but necessary for personal growth. It's in these moments of self-assessment that we uncover our blind spots and develop crucial self-awareness. We start to understand where our assumptions were flawed and where we need to improve our strategies and our understanding of ourselves.

Please keep in mind that setbacks often highlight weaknesses or areas needing improvement, providing crucial feedback for future endeavors. Analyzing a failed project, for instance, might reveal a lack of specific skills or resources. This recognition leads to focused learning and development, strengthening the overall skillset. This iterative process of improvement from setback to analysis to adjustment is essential for sustained progress.

Another valuable tool is seeking feedback from trusted mentors or colleagues. An external perspective can offer valuable insights that we might have overlooked during our self-reflection. A fresh perspective can illuminate blind spots, identify potential biases, and offer constructive criticism that helps us understand the situation more comprehensively. Don't hesitate to reach out and seek guidance when faced with a setback, it's a sign of strength, not weakness.

It's also essential to remember that the definition of a setback is subjective. What constitutes a significant setback for one person might be a minor inconvenience for another. Perspective plays a significant role.

Maintaining a balanced perspective, acknowledging both the significance of the setback and your overall progress, is critical. Celebrate your resilience and your capacity to learn and adapt, and remember that even significant setbacks don't negate past successes or diminish your future potential.

Finally, learning from setbacks necessitates patience and self-compassion. Growth isn't instantaneous, it's a gradual, iterative process. Don't expect to overcome every obstacle effortlessly. Embrace the process of learning, forgive yourself for mistakes, and remember that setbacks are an inherent part of the journey toward success. The resilience you develop by navigating these challenges is a testament to your strength and character. It is this journey, with its successes and setbacks, that truly defines your experience and builds your capacity for ongoing growth. The lessons learned along the way are often the most valuable assets in your arsenal, providing a foundation for greater resilience and future success.

Staying Committed to Your Journey

Staying committed to your journey of personal growth is not a sprint, it's a marathon. It requires sustained effort, unwavering dedication, and a deep understanding of your motivations. The path is rarely linear, it's filled with twists, turns, and unexpected obstacles. Maintaining momentum over the long haul demands strategies beyond simply setting goals, it necessitates nurturing a mindset of resilience and self-compassion.

One of the most powerful tools for maintaining long-term commitment is cultivating a strong sense of purpose. Why are you embarking on this journey? What are you hoping to achieve? What do you think are the rewards that await you? A clear understanding of your "why" fuels your determination, particularly during challenging times. When faced with setbacks, revisit your purpose. Remind yourself of the reasons you started, the vision you hold, and the person you aspire to become. This reconnection strengthens your resolve and provides the impetus to keep moving forward.

Self-compassion is equally crucial. Progress is not always steady, there will be days when you feel overwhelmed, discouraged, or even tempted to give up. In these moments, treat yourself with the same kindness and understanding you would offer a friend facing similar challenges. Avoid self-criticism and self-judgment. Instead, acknowledge your efforts, appreciate your progress, and remind yourself that setbacks are a normal part of the journey. Self-compassion fosters resilience, allowing you to bounce back from adversity and maintain your commitment to personal growth.

Regular self-reflection is another essential component of staying committed. Periodically assess your progress, celebrate your achievements, and honestly evaluate areas that need to be improved. This process should not feel like a judgment, rather, it should be an opportunity for learning and growth.

What strategies have worked well? Which ones need adjustment? What new skills or knowledge might enhance your progress? This ongoing assessment helps you refine your approach, stay on track, and adapt to changing circumstances.

Visualizing your desired outcome is also a highly effective technique. Create a vivid mental picture of your future self, embodying the qualities and achievements you desire. Imagine the feeling of accomplishment, the sense of pride, and the positive impact your growth will have on your life and those around you. This mental imagery strengthens your motivation, providing a powerful incentive to persist in the face of challenges. I'd like you to regularly revisit this visualization to rekindle your enthusiasm and reaffirm your commitment.

Breaking down your goals into smaller, manageable steps is equally important. Significant, overarching goals can feel daunting, leading to feelings of overwhelm and discouragement. By dividing your goals into smaller, more achievable steps, you create a sense of momentum and accomplishment. Each small victory reinforces your belief in your ability to succeed, fostering a positive feedback loop that motivates you to continue. Celebrate each milestone, no matter how small. Acknowledge your progress and appreciate the efforts you've made.

Building a support system is another key strategy. Share your goals with trusted friends, family members, or mentors who can provide encouragement, support, and accountability. Discuss your progress, challenges, and triumphs. Their encouragement can help you stay motivated and overcome obstacles. Seeking feedback and advice from others can provide fresh perspectives and valuable insights. A strong support network provides a safety net and reinforces your commitment to your journey.

Maintaining a healthy lifestyle also contributes significantly to your ability to stay committed. Prioritize sufficient sleep, regular exercise, and a nutritious diet. These fundamental aspects of well-being directly impact your energy levels, mood, and resilience. When your physical and mental well-being are supported, you are better equipped to handle stress, overcome challenges, and maintain your focus on your goals.

Moreover, incorporating mindfulness practices into your daily routine can enhance your ability to stay committed. Mindfulness involves paying attention to the present moment without judgment. This practice can reduce stress, increase self-awareness, and improve emotional regulation. By cultivating mindfulness, you develop a greater capacity to handle setbacks, stay focused on your goals, and maintain your commitment to personal growth.

Remember, the journey of personal growth is a lifelong endeavor. It's not about reaching a destination, it's about the continuous process of learning, evolving, and becoming the best version of yourself. Embrace the journey with self-compassion, celebrate your progress, and never underestimate the power of small, consistent steps. By implementing these strategies, you can cultivate the resilience, determination, and inner strength necessary to maintain momentum and achieve long-term success. Your commitment is an investment in your future self, and the rewards are immeasurable.

Furthermore, it's essential to recognize that the definition of success is deeply personal. External metrics or societal expectations do not solely define it. True success lies in aligning your actions with your values, pursuing your passions, and living a life that is authentic to you. Stay true to your core values, nurture your strengths, and embrace your unique talents. Remember that personal growth is a process of self-discovery, not a race to a predetermined finish line. Embrace the challenges, learn from setbacks, and celebrate the victories along the way. Your journey is unique and valuable, and your commitment to it is a testament to your strength and resilience.

Finally, remember to reassess your goals and adjust your strategies as needed regularly. Your priorities and aspirations may evolve, and it's perfectly acceptable to adapt your plans to align with your changing circumstances. Regularly reviewing your progress helps you stay focused, identify areas for improvement, and ensure that your goals remain relevant and meaningful. This process of continuous adjustment is a testament to your adaptability and your commitment to ongoing growth. The path to personal growth is dynamic and ever-evolving, and embracing this fluidity is crucial to maintaining your momentum and achieving long-term fulfillment. The journey itself, with its inherent ups and downs, is the very essence of the transformative experience. Embrace it thoroughly, and the rewards will be far more profound than any single achievement.

Living a Life of Purpose and Fulfillment

"Happiness is not something ready made. It comes from your own actions."

Dalai Lama

Living a life of purpose and fulfillment is the ultimate prize in the journey of self-improvement. It's not merely about achieving goals; it's about aligning your actions with your deepest values and aspirations. This alignment creates a sense of meaning and satisfaction that transcends the temporary highs and lows of daily life. It's the foundation upon which lasting happiness and contentment are built.

The path toward a life of purpose is rarely straightforward. It's a winding road full of unexpected detours and challenging climbs. Yet, it is precisely these challenges that sculpt our character, strengthen our resilience, and deepen our understanding of ourselves. Each obstacle overcome, each setback learned from, brings us closer to a more prosperous, more meaningful existence.

One of the most critical aspects of living a purposeful life is self-awareness. Understanding your strengths, weaknesses, values, and passions is paramount. This requires honest self-reflection, a willingness to confront uncomfortable truths, and a commitment to continuous self-discovery. Journaling, meditation, and mindful introspection can all be invaluable tools in this process. Consider engaging in activities that allow you to explore different facets of your personality, push your boundaries, and discover hidden talents.

Identifying your core values is equally crucial. What principles guide your decisions and actions? What is truly important to you? Are you living in accordance with these values? Often, we drift away from our core principles, distracted by external pressures and societal expectations. Taking time to reconnect with our values provides a compass, guiding us toward a life that aligns with our authentic selves. This alignment is a powerful source of intrinsic motivation, fueling our perseverance through challenges and setbacks.

Once you've gained clarity on your values and passions, the next step is to identify your life purpose. What contribution do you want to make to the world? What impact do you wish to leave behind? Your purpose doesn't need to be grand or world-altering; it can be something as simple as making a positive difference in the lives of those around you. The key is to find something that resonates deeply within you, something that ignites your passion and motivates you to strive for excellence.

Developing a clear vision for your future is essential for maintaining momentum. This vision isn't simply a list of goals; it's a vivid and inspiring picture of your ideal life, encompassing your personal, professional, and relational aspirations. Regularly revisiting this vision helps you stay focused, motivated, and connected to your purpose. It serves as a beacon, guiding you through the inevitable storms and setbacks that life throws your way.

Building strong relationships is another integral component of a fulfilling life. Nurturing meaningful connections with family, friends, and colleagues provides support, encouragement, and a sense of belonging. These relationships offer a buffer against stress, loneliness, and isolation, contributing significantly to our overall well-being. Invest time in cultivating these relationships, fostering open communication, and demonstrating genuine care and compassion.

Maintaining a healthy lifestyle is not merely about physical fitness; it's about cultivating a holistic well-being that encompasses physical, mental, and emotional health. Prioritize regular exercise, a balanced diet, sufficient sleep, and mindful stress management techniques. These practices nurture your energy levels, resilience, and emotional stability, allowing you to navigate the challenges of life with greater ease and grace.

Continuous learning and personal growth are lifelong pursuits that are essential for maintaining a sense of purpose and fulfillment. Cultivate a mindset of lifelong learning, embracing new challenges, seeking new knowledge, and continually expanding your horizons. Engage in activities that stimulate your mind, challenge your assumptions, and broaden your perspectives. This continuous growth keeps your life vibrant and exciting and prevents stagnation.

Furthermore, cultivating gratitude is an invaluable practice for enhancing happiness and well-being. Regularly acknowledging and appreciating the positive aspects of your life fosters a sense of contentment and gratitude, shifting your focus away from negativity and scarcity. Expressing gratitude to others strengthens relationships and enhances social connections, contributing to a more meaningful and fulfilling life.

Embracing failure as a learning opportunity is a crucial aspect of personal growth. Setbacks and challenges are inevitable; they are not indicators of failure but rather stepping stones toward success. Approach these experiences with a growth mindset, analyzing what went wrong, extracting valuable lessons, and adapting your approach accordingly. This resilience and adaptability are essential for maintaining momentum and achieving long-term fulfillment.

Finally, remember to celebrate your successes, both big and small. Acknowledging your accomplishments, no matter how modest, reinforces your sense of self-efficacy and motivates you to continue striving toward your goals. Take time to savor your victories, appreciating the effort and dedication that led to them. This positive reinforcement strengthens your commitment to your journey and reinforces your belief in your ability to achieve your aspirations. The journey of self-discovery and personal growth is a continuous process, not a destination. Embrace the challenges, learn from your mistakes, celebrate your successes, and continuously strive to become the best version of yourself. The rewards of living a life of purpose and fulfillment are immeasurable, enriching every aspect of your existence. This is a journey of continuous growth, and the commitment to this journey is what truly defines success. Remember to be kind to yourself along the way. Celebrate every milestone, no matter how small, and never underestimate the power of your resilience. The path to a fulfilling life is a personal one, and your unique journey is what makes it so valuable.

Keep Rising

You've come this far—through the doubts, the setbacks, the uncertainty, and the long silences of growth.
This book was never about fixing you. It was always about reminding you: You were never broken.

Every chapter, every exercise, every quiet moment of reflection has been a step—not toward perfection, but toward presence.
Toward wholeness.

You are not here to have it all figured out.
You are here to keep showing up.
To keep learning.
To keep rising.

So when the next challenge comes—and it will—you'll remember: Progress isn't loud. It's consistent.

One step. Then another.

That's how we move forward.
That's how we rise.

You are unshakable.

Acknowledgments

This book is born from a path I never expected to walk and from a strength I never knew I had.

To my family, my unwavering source of love and support, thank you for walking beside me through the darkest nights and celebrating with me in the light. Your faith in me gave me the strength to keep going, even when I had none left for myself.

To the doctors, nurses, and caregivers who guided me through my healing. Your compassion, precision, and humanity are part of every word on these pages. You reminded me that resilience isn't only about fighting but also about trusting, resting, and rising again.

To my friends, colleagues, and mentors, thank you for encouraging my voice, for believing in the message, and for reminding me that no one moves forward alone.

To every reader holding this book: may it meet you where you are and move with you where you're going. Your story matters. Your steps matter. And your strength, even if quiet, is unshakable.

Thank you for being part of this journey.

Author Biography

Dr. Ali Hamzeh Chalhoub is a technology leader, innovator, and survivor, whose journey through personal and professional challenges has shaped his unwavering belief in the power of resilience. With a PhD in Technology and Innovation Management, Engineering Management, he has spent years leading change, building systems, and helping people solve complex problems in high-pressure environments.

But his greatest transformation started far from the workplace during his battle with cancer.

What started as a fight for survival became a profound journey of self-discovery, healing, and purpose. From hospital rooms to boardrooms, Dr. Chalhoub learned that strength isn't found in perfection. Instead, it's built through perseverance, mindset, and small steps forward.

In *Unshakable*, he shares the lessons, tools, and reflections that helped him rise and can help you rise, too.

Dr, Chalhoub is the founder of Innovation Technology Engineering, LLC, and continues to mentor individuals and teams in personal growth, leadership, and resilience.

Back Cover Blurb for *Unshakable*

Even storms bow to steady steps.

Life doesn't come with guarantees. It brings uncertainty, setbacks, and unexpected storms. But in every challenge lies the opportunity to rise—not all at once, but steadily, powerfully, and on your own terms.

Unshakable is your guide to rebuilding from the inside out. It's not about perfection or instant change—it's about small steps that build lasting strength. Through personal insight, psychological tools, and powerful reflections, this book will help you:

- ✅ Break down overwhelming goals into simple, meaningful actions
- ✅ Reframe failure, fear, and self-doubt into momentum
- ✅ Create habits that support your growth—even on your hardest days
- ✅ Reconnect with your purpose and values
- ✅ Cultivate a mindset that moves you forward—no matter what

Whether you're healing, restarting, or just trying to keep going, *Unshakable* will remind you of what's possible:

You don't need to have it all figured out.

You just need to keep moving forward.